Freshwater Aquariums
in Your Life

Welcome to

Critter Press

Critter Press
A Simon & Schuster
1633 Broadway
New York, NY 1001

Copyright © 1997 b

Freshwater Aquarium
Freshwater Aquarium
in 1997.

All rights reserved. N
form or by any mear
ing or by any inform
ing from the Publish

MACMILLAN is a

ISBN 0-87605-433-

Cataloging-in-Public
the Library of Congr

Manufactured in the

10 9 8 7 6 5 4

SERIES DIRECTOR: A
ASSISTANT DIRECTOR
ILLUSTRATION BY BR
BOOK DESIGN BY MI
COVER DESIGN BY A
PRODUCTION BY KAT
STEPHANIE HAMMET
CHRIS VAN CAMP

Photography:
Front and back cover
Aaron Norman: 2–3,
    40, 43, 44, 45, 46
    64, 65, 67, 68, 69
Fred Rosenzweig: 22,
B. Everett Webb: 24,

part one
Welcome to the World of the

Freshwater Aquarium

External Features of a Freshwater Fish

Eye

Nostril

Mouth

Gill Cover

Pectoral Fin

Dorsal Fin

Pelvic (Ventral) Fin

Anal Fin

Caudal (Tail) Fin

Scales

About
Freshwater Fish

The world of fish is both fascinating and complex. This book will help you understand this world and teach you what you need to know to successfully set up and maintain a freshwater aquarium. This requires a general knowledge of fish, their anatomy and biology, as well as a thorough under-

standing of their proper care and husbandry. First, we will take a look at fish anatomy and what makes these animals so unique. Then we'll examine the aquarium and the importance of meeting the biological needs of fish.

Fish Evolution

Fish have evolved for over 400 million years to be the most numerous and diverse of the major vertebrate groups. There are well over 20,000 known species of fish that currently inhabit the earth and many more are being discovered every year.

Since salt water covers over 70 percent of the earth's surface and fresh water only 1 percent, one would expect that there would be many more marine (saltwater) species than freshwater species of fish. Actually, 41 percent of the world's fish species inhabit strictly freshwater. Although quite similar in many ways to their marine counterparts, the freshwater fish have adapted to a much wider range of habitats and to a greater variety of water conditions.

Fish Biology

There are no less than 8,000 kinds of freshwater fish, yet all fish have some common attributes. Since water is 800 times denser than air, fish have developed a variety of ways to move easily, breathe and feed in this dense medium. The biological adaptations involved include the body shape, fins, scales and swim bladder.

Forty-one percent of the world's fish species inhabit freshwater, like this Leopard Corydoras.

Body Form

A great deal can be learned about a species of fish by looking at its body form or shape. Fish that are streamlined or bullet shaped are specially adapted to open waters while flat or stocky fish are well adapted for living on or close to the bottom.

Fins

Almost all species of fish have fins in one form or another. The fins are critically important appendages which allow the fish to propel, stabilize, maneuver and stop. In some cases, fins have developed to protect the fish as well. Again, depending on the type of fish and the habitat it lives in, the fins can take on many shapes and functions. Bottom, sedentary, or slower moving fish possess rounded fins while faster, open water fish generally have longer, pointed fins.

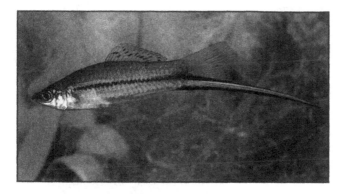

Fish with streamlined body shapes, like this Swordtail, are adapted to open waters.

Fins can be either paired or unpaired depending on species and function. The **pectoral** fins are the paired fins closest to the head. These fins act to help the fish stabilize, turn, maneuver, hover and swim backwards. The **pelvic** fins are also paired and in general act as brakes while aiding in stabilizing and turning the fish. The **dorsal** and **anal** fins are unpaired fins that may be elongated or short, elaborate or simple, singular or multiple. In some species of fish, the dorsal or anal fin may be completely lacking. Both fins help stabilize the fish and keep it moving straight. The **caudal** or **tail** fin is a single fin largely responsible for propelling the fish forward. This fin can also assist in turning and braking. Faster fish have deeply forked caudal fins while many deep-bodied and bottom fish have square or rounded tails.

Fish Anatomy

There are thousands of different species of fish, all uniquely adapted to their particular environments. However, most share fundamental characteristics that allow them to be classified together as fish.

Gills: These enable the fish to take in oxygen from the water.

Fins: These move the fish through the water, providing propulsion and steering.

Swim Bladder: This organ fills up with air, thereby controlling the fish's level in the water column.

Lateral Line: This sensory organ alerts the fish to movement close by. Helps fish in schools to move in synchronization.

Scales: These streamline and protect the body of the fish as it moves through the water.

In general, the main supporting structures of fish fins are soft rays. However, anyone who has handled a fish knows that the dorsal, anal or pectoral fins of many species also have spines. These sharp bony structures provide protection against predators.

Scales

The bodies of most tropical fish are covered with scales. The scales are composed of a hard bony substance and serve to protect the fish, reducing the chance of injury and infection. Covering the scales is a very thin layer of epidermal tissue that contains mucous cells. These cells produce the slimy texture that we normally attribute to fish. The mucous coating not only protects the fish against injury and infection but helps the fish swim more easily in the water, reducing friction between the body and water.

The scales of a fish are actually translucent and lack color. The source of the vibrant colors of tropical fish comes from

specialized pigment cells called **chromatophores** in the dermal layer of the skin. (Fish that are clear, like the Glassfish, lack these pigments.) The color of the fish depends on the types of chromatophores present.

Swim Bladder

Most species have a special organ called the swim bladder. This gas-filled sac located in the abdominal cavity of the fish acts as a life vest,

This Black Laced Angelfish has a three-chambered swim bladder that helps it to maintain the proper level in the water column.

keeping the fish at the correct level in the water column. There are many types of swim bladders and different methods fish use to fill the swim bladder with air. Some have a direct connection between the esophagus and the bladder and simply swallow air to fill it. Others must rely on gas exchange from specialized blood vessels in the circulatory system to fill the bladder.

In addition to its role in buoyancy control, the swim bladder also helps to mechanically amplify sound for better hearing in certain species of fish.

Feeding

A fish's mouth can tell you something about its feeding habits. Bottom feeders have downward pointing mouths, while surface feeders have mouths that point upward. For most fish, the mouth is at the end of the snout. The size of the mouth is usually directly related to the size of the fish's preferred food. For example, large predatory fish like Oscars have larger oval mouths for consuming smaller fish. On the other hand, fish that normally feed on small aquatic invertebrates, like Neon Tetras, have smaller mouths. Some tropical freshwater fish have specialized mouths for specialized feeding strategies. Plecostomus fish, for example, have special sucking type mouths for bottom feeding.

Freshwater tropical fish have a relatively straightforward digestive system which varies from species to species. In general, food passes from the mouth, down the esophagus, to the stomach, small and large intestines, and the waste products are expelled through the anus. However, several species lack true stomachs and instead have elongated, supercoiled intestines.

> **The Fishkeeper's Responsibilities**
>
> The fishkeeper (that's you) has an obligation to care for the fish he or she has brought home. Because the fish are contained in an artificial environment, it is up to you to establish and maintain their living space in an appropriate manner. The fishkeeper is responsible for providing:
>
> - high water quality
> - proper feeding
> - correct water temperature
> - a balanced fish community of the proper density
> - appropriate habitat and shelter
> - sufficient lighting
>
> Make sure you are ready to accept these responsibilities and the daily chores that go with them before you start setting up your aquarium.

Breathing

Among the most primary of the basic needs of fish is oxygen. Fish derive oxygen from water and have specialized organs, called **gills** that allow them to do so. Gills supply oxygen and remove carbon dioxide from the blood of the fish. Oxygen is then transported by the blood to the tissues where it is used to produce energy.

Most fish have four gills on each side of the head protected by a single gill flap, or **operculum.** When a fish breathes, water is taken into the mouth and passed over the gills and out the operculum. As water passes over the membranes and filaments of the gills, oxygen is removed and carbon dioxide is excreted. The gills have a very high number of blood vessels that deliver the oxygen to the rest of the fish.

Aside from the notable exceptions outlined above, fish typically possess the general circulatory, digestive, respiratory and nervous system features common to most vertebrates.

Senses

With few exceptions, fish have no less than five senses which they use to feed, avoid predators, communicate, and reproduce.

Fish's eyes are similar to our own in many ways, but they do lack eyelids. (Tinfoil Barb)

SIGHT

The eyes of most fish lack eyelids and their irises work slowly. Rapid changes in light intensity tend to shock a fish, a fact which should be taken into account by the aquarist. Gradual changes in light allow the fish to accommodate and avoid temporary blindness. The location of the spherical lenses of fish eyes renders most fish nearsighted. Depending on species, fish can detect color.

SOUND

Sound is conducted much farther and faster in water than in air. Most fish have an inner ear structure not noticeable on the outside of the fish. The auditory component of the inner ear consists of the **sacculus** and the **lagena,** which house the sensory components of hearing, the **otoliths.** Sound vibrations pass through the water, through the fish and reverberate the otoliths in the inner ear. Hearing is an integral component in the life of a fish.

SMELL

A fish has external nasal passages called **nares** that allow water to pass into and out of the olfactory organ located above its mouth and below its eyes. Water flows through the nares and into the olfactory pits where odors are perceived and communicated to the brain via a large nerve. The olfactory system remains isolated from the mouth and gills. For fish, smell is particularly important in prey and mate detection.

TASTE

This sense in fish is especially helpful in the identification of both food and noxious substances. In addition to being in the mouth, the taste buds are located on several external surfaces like their skin, lips and fins. Catfish have specialized barbels that possess taste buds and help them to detect food items in murky waters.

TOUCH

Fish have very specialized organs comprising the lateral line system that allow them to detect water movements. Sensory receptors lying along the surface of the fish's body in low pits or grooves detect water displacement. The lateral line is easily visible along the sides of most fish. This unique system helps the fish detect other fish and avoid obstacles.

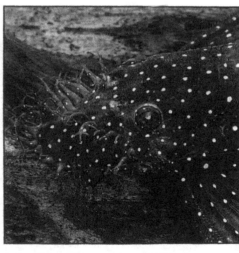

Catfish, like this Bristlenose Catfish, have barbels covered with taste buds that help them to locate food.

Setting Up the Tank:

Inside and Out

The Right Tank

Determine beforehand where you are going to put the aquarium. To avoid excess algal growth, do not place the aquarium in direct sunlight. Make sure that the structure the aquarium will rest on will hold the weight of the full aquarium. Water weighs about 8.4 pounds per gallon, so a 30-gallon tank will weigh at least 250 pounds when full. Choose a location that has an adequate electrical supply and is not too far from a source of water. Well-used living areas provide excellent settings for aquariums because the fish acclimate to people entering and leaving the room. Lastly, choose a location that can tolerate a water spill. Even the most meticulous of aquarists will spill water around an aquarium, and in many cases water will be splashed from a tank.

What Size Tank?

The general rule of thumb is to buy the largest aquarium that you can afford and accommodate in your home. Fish require adequate space to swim and sufficient oxygen to live; both are dictated by the size of the tank. The oxygen content of water is related to the surface area of the tank and the temperature of the water. Warmer water has less oxygen than colder water. Since most freshwater tropical fish prefer water warmer than 75 degrees Fahrenheit, the amount of oxygen may be limited in the tank. The more surface area a tank has, the more room for gas exchange at the surface—more opportunity for oxygen to enter the water and toxic gases to leave. Therefore, the larger the surface area of the tank, the more fish the tank can hold.

The number of fish you can keep in your aquarium is also determined by the surface area of your tank. Calculate the surface area of the tank by multiplying the length times the width. This number will tell you the maximum inches of fish your aquarium can accommodate. Most fishkeepers generally feel that 1 inch of coldwater fish requires 30 square inches of surface area and that 1 inch of warmwater fish requires 12 square inches of surface area. (Coldwater fish generally have higher oxygen requirements than tropical fish, thus the difference in requirements.) Of course, you will probably want to mix several species of fish of varying lengths in the tank. The minimal starter tank should be 20 gallons.

Because surface area is so important to the capacity and health of your aquarium, long tanks are much better than tall tanks. Even though both tanks may hold the same volume of water, the upright (tall) tank will have a much lower carrying capacity of fish because of its smaller surface area.

Next, decide on the tank itself. Most home aquariums are constructed of rectangular glass plates sealed with a silicone rubber cement. These are the most practical aquariums to buy for the beginner. They are nontoxic with glass that does not scratch as easily or yellow as acrylic does. When choosing your tank, be sure that there are no scratches on the glass and that there are no gaps in the silicone that may cause leakage.

A brief mention of the fish bowl will hopefully prevent the beginner from buying one. The confined, inhumane fish bowl is not a proper environment for a fish, whether its a goldfish or any other freshwater fish. Water in a fish bowl is unfiltered, not properly aerated, and very poorly maintained. A fish bowl is no more an aquarium than a closet is a house.

The Aquarium Stand

The best support for the heavy weight of the aquarium and all its components is a commercially manufactured aquarium stand. This type of support is built to hold a full aquarium. Homemade stands and other furniture may look sturdy, but can fail under the heavy load.

If you don't buy a commercially built stand, it is recommended that you place a $^5/_8$-inch sheet of plywood and a $^1/_2$-inch sheet of polystyrene cut to the dimensions of the tank under the tank.

The Hood

An essential item for any aquarium is a hood or cover. This prevents unwanted items from entering the tank and injuring the fish, keeps overzealous fish from jumping out of the tank, prevents water from splashing to the walls and floor and slows the rate of water evaporation from the tank. Water will condense on the cover and reenter the tank instead of evaporating, which reduces the necessity of adding more water. The hood also helps the aquarium retain heat, thereby reducing the use of the heating unit. Lastly, the hood keeps water from damaging the aquarium light and prevents a potentially dangerous electrical problem.

The hood is generally fitted to the dimensions of the tank and is adjustable to allow for aquarium accessories. It should be composed of thick ($^1/_8$-inch) glass or plastic so that it can support the weight of other aquarium components if needed. It should be segmented so that the entire assembly need not be removed to feed the fish or work in the tank. For the beginner, I strongly recommend the type of hood that also contains the aquarium light. These units are self-contained and designed to keep water from the lighting unit, minimize danger, and cover the entire tank. If possible, the tank, stand, and hood should be purchased as a package from a single manufacturer. This prevents the problem of mismatching aquarium components and may also be less expensive.

Creating Proper Water Conditions

The most important requirement of healthy fish is clean water. Fish in a natural environment are generally exposed to an open system of freshwater continuously; products of respiration and digestion are swept away and naturally filtered. In contrast, fish housed in the aquarium live in a closed system where products of respiration and digestion remain until they are removed. The fishkeeper must take responsibility for removal of these wastes and maintaining clean water. The piece of equipment that removes toxic substances from the aquarium is the filter.

Freshwater fish have adapted to a wide variety of habitats around the world. The water in each of these places has its own chemical characteristics to which the species of fish living there have adapted. These characteristics of water include pH (acidity level), hardness (mineral content), temperature, and oxygen content. In many cases, fish that have adapted to a specific temperature or pH cannot readily live under different conditions.

pH refers to the amount of acidity of the water. The pH scale ranges from 0 to 14 with a pH of 7 being neutral, a pH of 1 being very acidic and a pH of 14 being very alkaline. pH is influenced by a variety of factors including the amount of carbon dioxide and fish wastes in the water. In general, the beginner's aquarium pH should be between 6.5 and 7.5. Commercial test kits that are very simple to use are available at most pet stores. The pH level should be monitored every week or two to detect any changes. An abrupt drop in pH may be indicative of an increase in carbon dioxide or fish wastes. An increase in aeration or partial water change may alleviate the problem.

Water Hardness

The amount of dissolved mineral salts, namely calcium and magnesium, in the water is referred to as its hardness. Water with high concentrations of salts is referred to as "hard," while low levels create "soft" water. The degree of hardness scale (dH) ranges from 0 to over 30 degrees with 4–8 degrees being soft water and 18–30 degrees being hard water. Most freshwater fish do best in water between 3 and 14 degrees of hardness. The beginner generally does not need to alter water hardness unless the local tap water is excessively hard or soft. Commercial kits are now available to test and alter the degree of water hardness. These too can be purchased at the your pet store.

The Nitrogen Cycle

Fish are living creatures that obtain energy from food and burn that energy with the help of oxygen they breathe from the water. However, these processes generate waste products that are returned to the environment via the gills and the anus. These wastes are primarily carbon dioxide and nitrogenous compounds like ammonia. In the aquarium, these wastes must be removed. Carbon dioxide generally leaves the water through aeration at the surface or through photosynthesis by aquarium plants. Toxic nitrogenous compounds are converted to less toxic compounds via the nitrogen cycle.

In nature, the nitrogen cycle involves the conversion of toxic nitrogenous wastes and ammonia into harmless products by bacterial colonies. In short, species of bacteria convert solid wastes excreted by fish into ammonia, ammonia into nitrite and nitrite into nitrate. Nitrate is then utilized by plants as fertilizer and removed from the water. A healthy aquarium depends greatly on the nitrogen cycle to reduce toxic ammonia into less toxic nitrogen compounds.

Filter Systems

In natural systems, nitrogen compounds are readily removed from the fish's habitat. In the aquarium, this is accomplished by the filtration system. There are three basic types of filtration: mechanical, chemical and biological.

Mechanical filters physically remove suspended particles from the water by passing it through a fine filter medium, which sifts out the particles. External power filters and canister filters provide rapid mechanical filtration. **Chemical filtration** involves the chemical treatment of water to remove toxic substances. When you add activated carbon to an external power filter, you are providing chemical filtration. **Biological filtration** utilizes the nitrogen cycle to remove toxic compounds from the water. An excellent example of a biological filter is the undergravel filter, which draws water through the aquarium substrate. This substrate contains the necessary bacteria to convert nitrogenous wastes to nitrate. Although this type of filtration requires a bit more time to establish a viable working bacteria colony, it provides the best kind of filtration.

Tank Tips

The following are some basic things to keep in mind when choosing your aquarium tank.

- choose the largest tank you can afford and accommodate
- choose a long rectangular tank rather than a tall one
- never use a goldfish bowl
- choose glass rather than acrylic
- make sure there are no gaps in the sealant

Most commercially manufactured aquarium filters provide all three kinds of filtration. For example, the external power filter will mechanically remove particles, chemically remove toxins if it contains activated carbon and biologically convert nitrogenous wastes via the nitrogen cycle in its filter media.

Some types of filters available to the beginner include the internal box filter, the external power filter, the external canister filter and the undergravel filter. Here is a brief description of each type along with the pros and cons.

INTERNAL BOX FILTER

The internal box filter sits inside the aquarium. An external air pump drives air through the box drawing water from the aquarium through fibrous filter media and activated charcoal. Layers of filter media provide mechanical and chemical filtration as well as adequate substrate for biological filtration. Because it is driven by air, this filter circulates and aerates the water. Nonetheless, in my opinion the box filter does not provide adequate levels of filtration for the average aquarium. Aquarists who start with a tank of 20 gallons or more should not use this type of filter system to provide filtration. It is simply too small to handle the waste and debris that accumulate in the tank and would have to be changed frequently.

EXTERNAL POWER FILTER

The external power filter is the easiest and least complicated filter system for the beginner aquarist to employ. These filters provide all three kinds of filtration and are specifically designed to turn over large amounts of water. The external power filter hangs on the side of the tank and is powered by its own motor. While it works on the same premise as the box filter, the power filter is much more efficient at removing wastes and debris from the tank. It does not need to be cleaned as frequently as the box filter. Newer models have specialized filter cartridges that make cleaning these filters extremely easy. In addition, various types of cartridges can be purchased to chemically alter water quality and correct water chemistry problems. Like the box filter, the power filter circulates the water, providing aeration.

The external canister filter is the next step up in power filters. This filter is much larger than the others and is designed to filter large tanks of 50 gallons or more. The canister filter is composed of a large jarlike canister that generally sits next to the tank. It contains filter media and activated carbon like the other filters but has a much more powerful motor for filtering large amounts of water. I only recommend this kind of filter for the aquarist with the larger tank.

UNDERGRAVEL FILTER

The undergravel filter is considered by many to be the most effective type of filter because it provides biological filtration.

This filter consists of a plastic plate that sits under the gravel of the tank. In essence, this filter uses the aquarium gravel itself as the filter media and provides excellent water circulation and aeration. The undergravel filter relies chiefly on the establishment of a healthy bacterial colony in the gravel. For this reason, certain kinds of gravel are required for this filter and a longer setup time of many weeks is necessary to establish bacterial colonies. However, once a healthy filtration system is established, this filter can be used for months without intense maintenance and cleaning. This system may be the most complicated for the beginner. Excessive debris in the aquarium can clog the filter bed and must be removed routinely. Aquarists who want to maintain live plants will find that this filter will destroy root systems. In addition, fish may disturb the substrate and upset the filtration bed as well. The novice would be better off with an external power filter before tackling the complexities of the undergravel filter system.

Aeration

Although most filters provide water circulation and aeration to the aquarium, it is a very good idea to have an external air pump moving air through one or more airstones in the tank. Fish need to have a lot of oxygen available for respiration. This is especially true for tanks that are at their fullest carrying capacity of fish. The air pump will increase circulation in the tank, promote oxygen exchange at the surface, increase the escape of carbon dioxide and carbon monoxide and free ammonia from the tank. In addition, this increase in circulation will act to mix all the aquarium levels so that a uniform temperature is maintained throughout the tank.

AIR PUMPS

There are two general air pump designs: the diaphragm type and the piston type. The former is much more common and provides enough maintenance-free usage for the beginner's aquarium. The piston pump, however, is more powerful and should be used in larger aquariums and if an undergravel filter and multiple airstones need to be powered. The size and power output of air pumps vary. Consult your local dealer to match your aquarium with the proper air pump.

AIRSTONES

The airstone is generally made of porous rock that allows air to pass through it, splitting the airstream into tiny bubbles. You want the bubbles to slowly travel to the surface and agitate the water. Commercially manufactured tank decorations that act as airstones can be purchased at almost any pet store. Make sure that these fixtures don't produce bubbles that are too large and race to the surface.

AIR HOSE

Your air pump and airstones will require an air hose to form the link between the two. This is plastic tubing that will deliver air from your pump to the airstone. This should fit snugly at all joints so that air does not escape from the system. Air leaks will reduce the efficiency of the system (filter, airstone) and may ultimately burn out the pump. Make sure that the tubing is manufactured for use in the aquarium; other grades may be toxic to fish.

If you intend to run multiple airstones or additional devices like filters from a single pump, you will need one or more air valves. These will enable air flow to be directed to multiple devices from a single pump. The use of several air valves will allow you to turn devices on and off as you see fit.

The Heater

The aquarium heater maintains your aquarium within a specific temperature range regardless of the room temperature. The species you will be keeping as a beginner will require that the aquarium temperature be maintained at 75 to 79 degrees Fahrenheit (24 to 26 degrees Celsius). However, this is entirely species dependent and you should consult your local pet dealer or a fish encyclopedia for specific temperature requirements. Obviously, you should not mix species that have very different temperature preferences.

The most common aquarium heater is the submersible glass tubular heater with a built-in thermostat. This heater attaches to the side of the tank and has external controls. Once it is properly set, it will automatically respond to changes in water temperature and turn on and off. Newer models have temperature dials that are preset by the manufacturer. The aquarist should double-check the accuracy of the dial with a thermometer.

You should place your heater close to an area of high circulation so that heated water can be rapidly and evenly distributed throughout the tank. This is usually near the filter system or the airstones. The fully submersible heater can be placed at the bottom of the tank so that heating convection can be optimized.

Heater size is largely dependent on the size of the aquarium. The general rule is 5 watts of power for every gallon of water. Thus, a 20-gallon tank would require a 100-watt heater. Many fishkeepers recommend that two heaters be used in aquariums over 50 gallons; this allows for a more even distribution of heat in the aquarium and will also maintain correct temperatures if one heater fails. The calculated wattage should be divided between the heaters (50 gallons would require two 125-watt heaters).

Please handle your heater with extreme care. Do not switch your submersible heater on until it is submersed in water. Keep all of your electrical components unplugged until the tank is completely set up and full.

Thermometer

In order to maintain your temperature at suitable levels, all aquarists need an accurate thermometer. There are two types of thermometers for the aquarium: the internal floating or fixed thermometer and the external stick-on thermometer. The former type tends to be more accurate since the latter has a tendency to read a couple of degrees too low. This piece of equipment is of the utmost importance yet does not cost a lot. I recommend two thermometers to allow you to carefully monitor your aquarium temperature as well as to compare the accuracy of each unit. Don't cut corners when it comes to maintaining water quality and water temperature.

Aquarium Lighting

Proper lighting provides illumination and promotes plant growth. Sunlight provides a natural setting but will also promote excessive algal growth and alter temperature. Instead, beginner aquarists should purchase a commercially manufactured aquarium light to illuminate the tank. By far the most common is the fluorescent light that fits snugly on top of the aquarium hood and evenly provides cool illumination. Check with your pet shop dealer regarding options for bulb color and size, and the wise possibility of getting an on/off timer switch for the light.

Red and blue flourescent light will enhance the colors of red and blue fish, like this Cardinal Tetra, and promote plant growth in your aquarium.

Inside the Tank

Since your community aquarium will feature a variety of fish from multiple habitats, it is best to create an aquascape that is pleasing to the human eye as well as pleasing to the fish. This will require a variety of components that meet the habitat needs of its inhabitants.

Gravel

The bottom substrate of your aquarium will consist of gravel. Gravel is a natural addition that provides anchorage to plants and other decorations and also provides a home for useful bacteria that power the nitrogen cycle and rid the aquarium of toxic wastes. The beginner should be careful when choosing a substrate for the new aquarium. Certain kinds of materials can alter the chemistry of the aquarium, creating water hardness problems. I recommend that the beginner not collect gravel or other aquarium fixtures from the wild, but rather purchase them from a pet dealer.

All aquarium stores sell gravel for the freshwater aquarium. Be sure not to purchase coral sand which is recommended for saltwater aquarium use only. Gravel comes in a variety of sizes ranging from coarse to very fine. If you intend to use an undergravel filter, the latter will clog it and compromise its effectiveness. It will also harm the mouths and digestive systems of bottom feeding fish. On the other hand, if grains are too large, fish that tend to dig will not be able to move the substrate. This is particularly important for breeding fish. A good medium pea-size gravel is well suited for the beginner's aquarium.

The gravel bottom of your aquarium provides anchorage for plants and decorations, and a home for beneficial bacteria. (Sail Fin Mollie)

The gravel should be about 1.5–2 inches deep on the aquarium bottom. If you use an undergravel filter, 2.5–3 inches is recommended. It is always best to buy a bit extra so that when you aquascape your tank, you have sufficient amounts to sculpture the bottom.

Plants

The first decision you must make in regard to plants is whether to add artificial or live plants to your aquarium. My personal feeling is that the beginner aquarist is faced with a variety of problems in the first year of maintaining an aquarium, and, therefore, the maintenance and nurture of live plants need not be added to the list of things that can go wrong. While live plants are more natural looking and provide an excellent service of reducing carbon dioxide and utilizing nitrates in the tank, they also have very specific needs that must be met. If proper care is not taken, they will die and contribute to water quality problems that you are desperately trying to avoid.

Decorations

Pet stores sell a variety of tank decorations that enhance the habitat you are providing your fish. By purchasing these tank decorations from the dealer, you are avoiding contaminating your tank with toxic substances and water chemistry–modifying agents. Slate and granite are excellent natural additions to the tank. Wood is an attractive addition to any tank, but this too should be purchased, rather than gathered, by the beginner.

A variety of tank decorations are available to enhance the appearance of your aquarium.

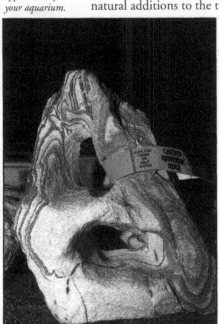

Take the time to design the kind of setting you want to build for your fish. In their natural habitats, fish have access to shelter as well as sufficient swimming space. Caves and rock ledges for the fish to hide in will mimic your fish's natural habitat and increase their sense of security and well-being.

Other Accessories

I have already mentioned the importance of **water quality test kits.** Make sure that when you purchase your complete aquarium setup that these are not left out. Test kits that measure pH, hardness, and nitrogen compounds are a must. Included in the latter should be tests for ammonia, nitrite and nitrate.

There are a couple of handy accessories that will help you keep your tank clean. An **algal sponge** or aquarium cleaner is a sponge attached to a long handle used for scraping down the inside of the tank without having to empty the aquarium out. The sponge will easily scrape off algae, but will not scratch the tank. A magnetic aquarium cleaner is also an effective cleaning tool. This uses two magnets with cleaning surfaces. One magnet is kept outside the tank and the other is controlled on the inside walls of the tank by the outside magnet.

An **aquarium vacuum** is a must for the beginner. This is usually a hand pump siphon that enables you to extract larger debris from the aquarium floor without having to submerse your hands or use a net.

You will definitely need a **fishnet** or two. It's better to have a couple of sizes handy depending on the size of your tank and the size of your fish. You will use a fishnet more than you think. It will come in very handy when you need to remove a fish that is ill or dead, or an aggressive fish, or when the time has come to clean the tank and remove all the fish.

Setting Up
the
Aquarium

The first step to properly setting up your new aquarium is to assemble all the components in the area where you want the aquarium to be. Remember to follow the guidelines in "Where to Place Your Tank" in chapter 2 when choosing the right place for your aquarium. Inventory the various pieces of the aquarium and make sure that you are not lacking any essential component. You don't want to be well into setting it up and find that you are missing something.

Successful Setup

Once you are confident that everything is in order, take the following steps to set up your aquarium.

1. Make sure everything is clean. Give the gravel, tank, filter, heater, aquarium decorations, artificial plants and anything else you expect to put in the tank a thorough rinsing with clean warm water. Residues, dirt and toxic agents can accumulate on your equipment between the time it is manufactured and the time it gets to your home. When it comes to cleaning aquarium decorations like rocks and wood, use a scrubbing brush to remove dirt. Never use any kind of soap when cleaning your aquarium components; this can cause immediate water quality problems.

Make sure you thoroughly clean any elements you will be placing in your aquarium, like these artificial corals.

Cleaning your gravel is a very important part of this process. Uncleaned gravel will add dust to the aquarium making it cloudy and unhealthy for its occupants. To clean gravel, empty it into a large container like a 5-gallon bucket and fill the container with water. Thoroughly agitate the water and stir the gravel before dumping out the water. Do this several times until the water that you pour off is clear. For new gravel, four to five rinsings is generally sufficient.

2. Place the tank on its stand exactly where you want it to reside. Do not expect to move the tank once it is filled with water. Now it is time to begin assembling the interior of your aquarium. Aquascape your tank beginning with the lowermost layer, the gravel. If you are going to use an undergravel filter, remember to add it before

gently pouring the gravel into the tank. Terrace the gravel so that it is higher in the back than in the front of the tank.

3. Add any larger pieces of rock, wood, etc. Don't attempt to add plants or smaller decorations until the water is added to the tank; they may be disrupted by the filling process. Remember to leave spaces for heaters, filters and other equipment.

4. This would be an appropriate time to add the airstones to the aquarium, taking the opportunity to conceal air supply tubing behind larger decorations.

5. Add water to the tank. To avoid disrupting your aquascape, place a clean plate or bowl on the substrate and pour the water onto it. If you suspect that your tap water is excessively hard or soft or contains high levels of chloramine, you may need to purchase water or chemically treat your tap water. In most cases, the aquarium aging process combined with filtration will alleviate minor tap water problems.

6. Place the filter and heater in the tank and position them. Prepare the former by following manufacturer instructions regarding filter media before setting it on or in the tank. Position the heater in such a way as to maximize its output. Place it near sources of water circulation like filter outlets or airstones.

7. Place the smaller decorations in the tank, add the thermometer, and fine tune your aquascape. Add artificial plants according to your plan.

8. Fit the hood, making sure that the external components and electrical equipment are properly placed. Add the light on top of the canopy and make sure it is hooked up correctly.

9. When you are confident that the electrical wiring is safely insulated from sources of water, plug the aquarium

---

Bringing Your Fish Home

When you bring your fish home, the pet dealer will put it in a plastic bag with water and enough oxygen for a short trip. Ask to have the plastic bag placed inside a dark opaque bag. Keeping the fish in the dark will help reduce the stress of the trip. You must resist the temptation to take the fish out and gawk at it. Bringing the fish from the dark into the light into the dark again can put the fish in shock. Keep it in the bag until you get home.

units in and turn on the system. Make sure the heater is properly adjusted, this may take a day or so. Check the operation of the filter, air pumps and light.

10. Let the tank water mature before adding any fish.

Fish require specific levels of water pH and hardness, so let your aquarium mature before adding your fish. (Leopard Angelfish)

Aquarium Maturation

To get a well-balanced, artificial habitat, you need to let the tank mature. Water circulation, temperature regulation and filtration will help your water mature in a relatively short period of time.

The estimated period of water conditioning varies depending on what kind of setup you have. The new undergravel filter will take between four and six weeks to fully establish itself. It depends on when your pH and hardness stabilize and how well you have established the nitrogen cycle. There are commercial treatments available that will accelerate the maturation process. If you decide to use one of these, get advice from your local dealer and read instructions carefully.

It is important to test your water daily to determine when you can add fish to the tank. In general, once pH and hardness have stabilized in two to four days, the next step is to fuel the nitrogen cycle. This can be done by introducing a few very hardy, inexpensive fish, like common goldfish, into the tank. These fish will produce the necessary ammonia that will help establish bacterial colonies that comprise the nitrogen cycle.

Once the fish have been introduced, it is important to continue to monitor ammonia, nitrite and nitrate levels. At first, within a few days, you will see ammonia and nitrite levels begin to climb rapidly and nitrate will remain low. If you have introduced the fish too soon, this can result in their being poisoned, a phenomenon known as "new tank syndrome." This means that the bacterial colonies that convert these compounds into the less harmful nitrate are not yet established. In most cases, if you wait a few days before introducing your starter fish, this will not occur.

Make sure your aquarium contains all the necessary elements and is chemically stabilized before you begin to add fish.

Gradually, in about one to two weeks, your ammonia levels will stabilize, nitrite will decrease and nitrate will increase. This is a sure sign that it is time to add more fish to your aquarium. Do this slowly, adding a couple of fish every few days. Remember to calculate the maximum number of fish that your tank can handle and use this number conservatively. Continue to monitor ammonia, nitrite, and nitrate levels throughout this period. If a sudden peak occurs in the former two, stop adding fish until that peak diminishes.

Adding Fish to the Tank

When you leave your pet store, you will most likely have your selected fish packed in plastic bags. Make sure the dealer fills the airspace in the bag with oxygen. Take care not to disturb or shock your fish during transport. Don't expose the bags to excessive changes of temperature or light, and don't bounce them around during the trip home. Follow these steps when you get home.

1. Float the plastic bag containing your fish in the tank so that the temperature in the bag can acclimate to that in the aquarium. Let it sit in the tank for at least ten to fifteen minutes.

2. Open the bag to let some fresh air in and seal it again. To insure that the fish will not be shocked by the aquarium water, make sure that both have a temperature within a degree of each other. Add a handful of water from your aquarium to the bag and let it sit for another ten to fifteen minutes.

3. Now you can add the fish to the tank by simply and gently inverting the bag into the tank, letting the fish out.

part two
Freshwater

Aquarium Fish

Common
Freshwater Fish Families

Congo Tetras

You are most likely to have freshwater tropical fish in your new aquarium. Although most are now bred in captivity for the aquarium trade, in their natural habitats they are found throughout the world. The diversity of these fish is amazing and can be daunting. In order to make freshwater fish easier to understand and sort out, scientists have classified them into different groups.

A particular species has a common name, which can differ depending on the region or the language. However, a species also has a scientific name that is used to identify that species in all languages. The scientific name of a species is based in Latin and is in two parts, the genus and the species. For example, the scientific name of the Neon Tetra is *Paracheirodon innesi* and the Cardinal Tetra is *Paracheirodon axelrodi*. The first name refers to the genus, or grouping of very similar species, to which both species belong. If you look at these fish, you can see that they are extremely similar. The second name refers only to that species and no other. Similar genera (plural for genus) are classified into families.

In general, most experts prefer to combine freshwater aquarium fish families into two major groups based on their reproductive biology: livebearers and egglayers. This is based purely on the method these fish use to reproduce. In the following section, I am going to outline the major families of each group. I have taken the liberty of grouping families that have similar characteristics. By no means is this a complete list of tropical freshwater fish families, only those you are most likely to encounter. When I indicate that a single species has additional varieties or strains, it refers to the method of selective breeding of a species for certain characteristics and establishing a new variety (not a new species). For example, the common goldfish, *Carassius auratus*, has been selectively bred to over 125 recognized varieties.

Guppies, like many other livebearers, are hardy fish that breed readily in captivity.

Livebearers

The livebearers include four major families (Anablepidae, Goodeidae, Hemirhamphidae and Poeciliidae) that are kept in captivity. These are the common aquarium fish known as guppies, mollies, platys and swordtails, as well as the various breeds and strains of each. These are especially hardy fish that breed readily in captivity. The males of these families are easily recognizable by their possession of a **gonopudium.** This modified pelvic fin is used by the male during mating with the female.

Egglayers

Barbs and Rasboras

These fish belong to the closely related families Cyprinidae and Cobitidae which contain over 1,300 species of fish. Loaches, very popular aquarium fish, fall into the latter group. Examples of these fish include the Tiger Barb from Indonesia, the Zebra Danio from India and the Clown Loach from India. The Red-tailed Shark, which is not a shark but actually a rasbora, is also a member of this family; it originates in Thailand.

Catfish

There are fifteen families and 2,000 species of catfish that contribute to the aquarium trade. The so-called armored catfish (Loricariidae, Callichthyidae), include the popular "plecostomus" fish and other algae eaters found in home aquariums. This group also includes the 140 species of *Corydoras* catfish with their large heads and short bodies. These South American catfish are known for their propensity to feed on the substrate, thereby cleaning the tank bottom. Other families include the banjo catfish, the naked catfish, the glass catfish, and the pim catfish. Most of these are peaceful and adapt easily to a community tank.

Characins

This group contains thirteen families of fish more commonly known as the tetras. There are over 1,300 species of tetras originating mostly in South America, but also Africa. Common characteristics of this group include the possession of a toothed jaw and an adipose fin or second dorsal fin. In many species, males can be distinguished from females by the possession of hooklike spines on the anal fin or projecting from the base of the tail. These fish are generally school forming in their natural habitat. Two of the most popular characins with very different dispositions are the Neon Tetra and the Red-bellied Piranha. A small school of the former is an attractive addition to the aquarium, but the latter belongs in a single species tank. Overall, most members of this group are peaceful and make excellent additions to the community aquarium.

Cichlids

The family Cichlidae contains over 900 species of fish originating from Central and South America, parts of the Caribbean, southern India and across Africa. Cichlids inhabit a wide range of habitats throughout these areas including salt water and high temperature water (104 degrees Fahrenheit). Most cichlids are small to medium-size with a single dorsal fin that is usually composed of hard and soft rays. Some species, like the freshwater angelfish, are compressed laterally and have long ornate fins. Temperament in this group ranges from pugnacious and intolerant to very peaceful. Care should be taken when selecting cichlids for the community aquarium. Common cichlids include the Jack Dempsey, oscar, angelfish and discus. A common behavior among many African Lake cichlids is mouthbrooding during which the female will take her fertilized eggs into her mouth until they hatch. Often the fry will return to her mouth for shelter. Cichlids can be extremely territorial and some mate for life.

This Red Oscar is a member of the cichlid family.

Killifish

These fish belong to primarily two families, the Aplocheilidae and the Cyprinodontidae. They are very diverse fish with more than 450 species spanning all the continents with the exceptions of Australia and Antarctica. Killifish have permeated salt, brackish and freshwater habitats throughout their range. Distinctive rounded scales and a lateral line system only on the area around the head are characteristic features of this group. Some of the more common members of this group include the lyretails, rivulus and lampeyes.

Labyrinth Fish

This group of four families is so-named for the special organ inside their head called the labyrinth. This organ allows the fish to breathe in air at the surface. The inhaled air is pressed into the labyrinth and the oxygen is drawn from it there. This enables these fish to live and survive in oxygen-depleted waters. Many of these fish come from Thailand, Indonesia, Cambodia, and Malaysia. The most popular of the labyrinth fish belong to the family Belontiidae, which includes the

Siamese Fighting Fish, like all other labyrinth fish, possess a special organ that allows them to breathe air at the surface.

Gouramis, Paradise Fish and Bettas. The Paradise Fish is extremely hardy, but becomes very territorial in an aquarium as an adult. The Betta is better known as the Siamese Fighting Fish, so-named because the males fight and tear their finnage to shreds. Although sometimes displayed in very small fish bowls, these fish should not be kept in less than a liter of water—they are very sensitive to temperature changes. The Gouramis are very popular additions to the community tank; they are peaceful fish with ornate fins that prefer heavy vegetation. The only member of the family Helostomatiidae maintained in captivity is the popular Kissing Fish. Native to Thailand, these fish are actually displaying aggression when "kissing" another member of the species.

Rainbowfish

This group is comprised of three families mostly originating from New Guinea and eastern Australia. Members of this group are peaceful, active, schooling fish with oval, laterally compressed bodies. A common member of this group is the Splendid Rainbow.

Knifefish

The unique group of knifefish is comprised of four families. The speckled knifefish (Apteronotidae), the banded knifefish

(Gymnotidae) and the American knifefish (Rhamphichthyidae) are found in Central and South America. The fourth family, Notopteridae, comes from the fresh waters of Africa and Asia. These fish are so-named for their laterally compressed, blade-shaped tapered body form. Most species are nocturnal and peaceful, but they should be kept with fish of similar size. Some of the Notopterid knifefish, however, are aggressive and are best kept alone.

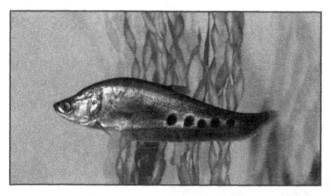

Knifefish, like this Clown Knifefish, got their name from their tapered, blade-shaped body form.

Mormyrids

Commonly known as the elephantnose fish, species of the family Mormyridae have mouths extended like an elephant's trunk. Found in Africa, these fish use this modified mandible as a sensory organ. They also possess an organ near their tail that generates weak electric signals. When an elephantnose becomes nervous, its electric pulse rate increases. The continuous pulsing of the electric organ can disturb other aquarium fish as well as other elephantnose fish.

Miscellaneous

There are at least forty families of fish kept in aquariums that I have not covered above. They are so diverse in form and behavior that discussion of each would require too much space. I thoroughly recommend that you consult one of the fish encyclopedias listed in the bibliography (chapter 10). These references not only describe each species available to the aquarist, but list the specific aquarium requirements of that species. Those groups of families that I have reviewed are those most commonly seen in pet stores.

Choosing

the Right Fish for Your Aquarium

Turquoise Rainbowfish

Throughout this book, I have referred to your aquarium as a community tank. The community tank contains different species of compatible fish, while the species tank contains only a single species of fish. I feel that the beginner should establish a community tank to start with; the species tank concept is best for those who want to maintain fish that require special tank conditions or are extremely aggressive.

The Best Aquarium Fish for Beginners

There are a wide variety of fish that are well suited for the community aquarium. The important thing to do is to balance the types of fish in your tank. There are fish that live in the topwater, the midwater and on the bottom. In the community tank, you want to recreate this kind of environment by having fish spread throughout the tank on every level.

In addition, many species of fish school by nature. This can be a very attractive addition to the community tank. These schooling fish should never be kept alone but rather in a group of at least five or six individuals.

As I mentioned earlier in the general overview, some fish tend to be aggressive. These should be avoided by the beginner because a single antagonistic fish in a community tank can wreak havoc on the other species.

Another aspect the novice will sometimes overlook is the maximum size of a particular species. A fish will grow continuously throughout its life. Some species grow faster than others. You don't want to put a fish in your tank that will attain a length of 12 inches in less than a year. This will not only disrupt your aquarium capacity, but the larger fish will undoubtedly dominate the tank. Some species are very compatible with other species when they are juveniles but become solitary and aggressive as adults. These fish do not belong in the peaceful community tank.

When your tank is fully established, the water chemistry has balanced, and you are ready to stock your aquarium, I thoroughly recommend that you have a game plan in mind. Don't blindly go to your pet dealer and look for fish to fill your tank. This can result in fish incompatibility. Instead, decide on the kind of fish you want to start with beforehand. Take some of my suggestions in this section. Consult with some of the fish encyclopedias listed in the bibliography. In other words, establish a good list of potential fish that you want to introduce into your aquarium. Remember to choose a variety of species that will live throughout the water column from the top to the bottom.

Be selective when you get to the pet store. Buy fish only from healthy looking aquariums with clear water, clean panes and no dead fish in the tank. Make sure that the fish you want is healthy looking. If the fish has any cuts, scrapes, or fin problems, don't buy it. Watch for possible symptoms of disease such as white granular spots, cottony white patches, frayed fins or dull skin. Watch the behavior of the fish. Healthy fish swim in a lively manner and are not shy.

Most fishkeepers agree that it is important to introduce your fish to the aquarium in batches, buying fish in lots every ten to fourteen days. This is important for the newly established aquarium. This allows fish to acclimate to each other and prevents aggressive behavior toward a single fish when it is introduced.

The following is a list of species that are particularly easy to take care of. They are well suited for the beginner's community tank where pH ranges from 6.5 to 7.5 and temperature is maintained between 75 and 79 degrees Fahrenheit. I have arranged these fish according to the part of your tank that they are most likely to inhabit: topwater, midwater and bottom.

Topwater Fish

The topwater fish are not restricted to the upper levels of the tank, but are more likely to be seen there. For these species, feeding and spawning, in particular, occur at or near the surface of the aquarium.

Guppy.

Guppy (*Poecilia reticulata*)
Family: Poeciliidae
Distribution: Central America to Brazil
Size: Males 1.5 inches, Females 2.5 inches
Food: Omnivorous
Temperature: 64 to 81 degrees Fahrenheit

This species is a definite favorite among beginners because it is a very hardy fish that gives birth to live young every month. The males are very colorful with ornate finnage and a gonopodium; females are dull in coloration. Selective breeding has resulted in the production of over one hundred varieties. These fish are vigorous swimmers preferring small groups of four to six members. Provide plenty of cover and floating plants and you may be able to successfully raise the fry.

Green Swordtail (*Xiphophorus helleri*)
Family: Poeciliidae
Distribution: Central America
Size: Males 4 inches, Females 4.5 inches
Food: Omnivorous
Temperature: 68 to 79 degrees Fahrenheit

Green Swordtail.

The Green Swordtail is another popular community fish because it breeds readily in captivity. The males possess a long swordlike extension on the lower part of their tail that develops as the fish matures (hence the species' common name). The males can be temperamental and will harass the females so it is best to have the females outnumber the males; males will quarrel with each other as well. These fish breed every twenty-eight days at 74 degrees Fahrenheit. Like the guppy, dense vegetation will provide cover for developing fry. Another benefit of this species is its tendency to consume algae.

Black Molly (*Poecilia sphenops*)

Family: Poeciliidae
Distribution: Mexico to Colombia
Size: 2.5 inches
Food: Omnivorous
Temperature: 64 to 82 degrees Fahrenheit

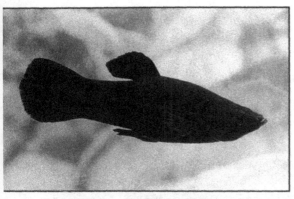

Black Molly.

The Black Molly is actually a hybrid of the original variety, the Mexican Molly. The many varieties prefer temperatures on the upper end of the range. Other varieties include the green, marbled, albino and lyretail mollies. This species is another livebearer that is gentle and basically a vegetable eater. Like the swordtail, the molly will consume aquarium algae keeping it in check. This species is lively and prefers small groups of four to six members. Although not as hardy as other livebearers, the molly will prosper if aquarium conditions are kept constant.

Red Wag Platy.

Platy (*Xiphophorus maculatus*)

Family: Poeciliidae
Distribution: Mexico and Guatemala to Honduras
Size: Males 4 inches, Females 4.5 inches
Food: Omnivorous
Temperature: 72 to 79 degrees Fahrenheit

The platy belongs to the same genus as the swordtail and is therefore a very close relative. Some consider it to be the ideal community fish. As with most livebearers, many color varieties have been commercially bred for the home aquarium. Plenty of cover in dense vegetation will lead to successful breeding and the survival of the fry in a community tank. The platy consumes algae and prefers to live in small groups of five to seven fish. A very similar species, the Variable Platy *(Xiphophorus variatus)* is equally as hardy and well suited for the community tank.

Zebra Danio *(Brachydanio rerio)*
Family: Cyprinidae
Distribution: India
Size: 2.5 inches
Food: Omnivorous
Temperature: 64 to 75 degrees Fahrenheit

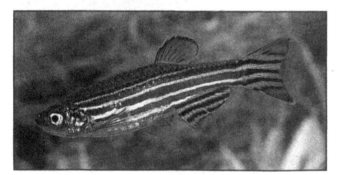

Zebra Danio.

The torpedo-shaped danios are very active schooling fish that should be kept in groups of at least seven or eight. This egglaying cyprinid has been commercially bred to both albino and long-finned strains. Males are generally slimmer than females and usually remain loyal to one female once they have spawned. This species likes to spend time at the surface where it is open and bright. A similar species is the Pearl Danio *(Brachydanio albolineatus)*.

White Cloud Mountain Minnow
(Tanichthys albonubes)
Family: Cyprinidae
Distribution: Southern China

*White Cloud
Mountain
Minnow.*

Size: 1.5 inches
Food: Omnivorous
Temperature: 64 to 72 degrees Fahrenheit

This very undemanding, active cyprinid fish should be kept in a group of eight or more. Males are slimmer and have more intense coloration than females. However, note that these peaceful fish prefer cooler water and should only be kept in temperatures less than 72 degrees Fahrenheit.

Common Hatchetfish *(Gasteropelecus sternicla)*
Family: Gasteropelecidae
Distribution: Brazil, Guyana, Surinam
Size: 2.5 inches
Food: Carnivorous
Temperature: 73 to 79 degrees Fahrenheit

*Silver
Hatchetfish.*

This surface dweller and its close relative the Marbled Hatchetfish *(Carnegiella strigata)* are characins that need to be kept in schools of at least six fish. The unusually deep body of these species makes them an interesting addition to any community aquarium. All hatchets are excellent jumpers so be sure to keep the hood in place on the tank. A few floating plants will provide adequate cover for these gentle fish.

Siamese Fighting Fish *(Betta splendens)*
Family: Belontiidae
Distribution: Cambodia, Thailand
Size: 3 inches
Food: Carnivorous
Temperature: 75 to 84 degrees Fahrenheit

Siamese Fighting Fish.

The beautiful labyrinth fish is a popular addition to the community aquarium. Selective breeding over the years has enhanced the brilliant ornate finnage of the males. However, only one male may be kept per aquarium, otherwise vicious fighting will occur; duels between males can result in death. Males are generally peaceful with other species unless they have similar fin veils. The smaller, shorter finned females are more drab but may be kept together in a community tank. This egglaying species builds a bubble nest at the surface of the aquarium where the eggs are guarded by the males.

Midwater Fish
Many of the midwater swimmers belong to the groups of fish referred to as the cyprinids and the characins; most do best in schools of eight or more individuals. With this in

mind, the beginner should consider only one or two species of schooling midwater fish.

Rosy Barb *(Barbus conchonius)*
Family: Cyprinidae
Distribution: Northern India
Size: 3 inches
Food: Omnivorous
Temperature: 64 to 72 degrees Fahrenheit

Rosy Barb.

Barbs get their name from the short threadlike barbels that act as sensory organs of touch on either side of their mouths and sometimes on their lips. Their vigor and agility in the midwaters of the tank contribute greatly to the vitality of the aquarium. Barbs, however, can cause harm to smaller fish and fish with ornate veil-like fins. The Rosy Barb is a very peaceful species that adapts well to a community aquarium. However, it prefers cooler water than other community fish and is most colorful in these conditions. A related species, the Tiger Barb *(Barbus tetrazona)* has a bit wilder disposition when introduced singly or as a pair. This fish will wreak havoc among other occupants, nipping fins and harassing them. However, if kept in schools of eight or more, they establish a hierarchy, and generally leave other fish alone. It is recommended that schools contain both the more colorful males and the heavier females. This Indonesian species prefers warmer water in the range of 68 to 79 degrees Fahrenheit. The Ruby Barb *(Barbus nigrofasciatus)* of Sri Lanka also prefers warmer water and, when in the company of other barbs, is a peaceful addition to the community tank.

Red Rasbora (*Rasbora heteromorpha*)

Family: Cyprinidae
Distribution: Southeast Asia
Size: 2 inches
Food: Omnivorous
Temperature: 72 to 77 degrees Fahrenheit

Red Rasboras.

This popular species is another schooling cyprinid that requires a group of eight or more fish to be at its best. Because of its size, it should be kept with other equally small and peaceful species. Males are distinguishable from females by a slightly rounded edge at the bottom of the black body marking. The Red Rasbora is deeper bodied than its close relative, the Red-striped Rasbora *(Rasbora pauciperforata)*, which is streamlined in shape. This species gets about an inch larger, has similar temperature preferences, and is ideal for the community aquarium when maintained in groups of eight or more. Egglaying species of rasboras are not as easy to breed as the barbs, but they are extremely peaceful.

Neon Tetra *(Paracheirodon innes)*

Family: Characidae
Distribution: Peru
Size: 1.5 inches
Food: Omnivorous
Temperature: 68 to 79 degrees Fahrenheit

Capable of tolerating a wide range of temperatures, this characin is considered by many to be the most popular of all aquarium fish. Like other midwater fish, the Neon Tetra should be kept in a school of six or more individuals. The iridescent coloration of this fish will glow if the tank is properly lighted. Related species, including the Cardinal Tetra *(Paracheirodon axelrodi)* and the Glowlight Tetra *(Hemigrammus erythrozonus)*, are also peaceful shoaling (schooling) fish that contribute greatly to a community tank. The Black Neon Tetra *(Hyphessobrycon herbertaxelrodi)* has a stouter body than the Neon Tetra and makes an ideal community fish as well. In all these species of tetra the males are generally slimmer than the females.

Black Neon Tetra.

Angelfish *(Pterophyllum scalare)*
Family: Cichlidae
Distribution: Central Amazon to Peru, Ecuador
Size: 6 inches
Food: Omnivorous
Temperature: 75 to 82 degrees Fahrenheit

The unique beauty of these fish is very appealing to the beginner, but you must have a well-established aquarium with constant water conditions. They cannot tolerate extreme fluctuations in water quality and temperature. Once you have established your aquarium and water quality remains constant, the introduction of this species is justified. These are placid fish that require tall decorations (like plants) among which they will stay quietly. They are best kept in small groups of four to six with other even-tempered fish like Neon Tetras and Black Mollies. The angelfish is one of the few cichlids that has a somewhat

Angelfish.

peaceful disposition. However, this species can get up to 6 inches long and will eat smaller fish at this size. The many varieties of angelfish come in a wide range of patterns and colors.

Blue Gourami
(*Trichogaster trichopterus*)

Family: Belontiidae
Distribution: Southeast Asia to Indo-Australian Islands
Size: 4 inches
Food: Omnivorous
Temperature: 72 to 82 degrees Fahrenheit

Blue Gourami.

The Blue Gourami and its relatives, the Dwarf Gourami *(Colisa lalia)*, the Snakeskin Gourami *(Trichogaster pectoralis)*, and the Pearl Gourami *(Trichogaster leeri)*, are peaceful labyrinth fish that do not need to be kept in groups but do quite well in pairs. Their elaborate finnage and various color forms warrant that care be taken not to include them with fin nippers like Tiger Barbs. Although listed here as midwater fish, the gouramis will swim among the bottom decorations and make frequent excursions to the surface. These egglayers build bubble nests during spawning like other labyrinth fish. The Paradise Fish *(Macropodus opercularis)* closely resembles the gouramis and is also a very hardy labyrinth fish that can tolerate temperatures down to 61 degrees Fahrenheit. This species may cause trouble, annoying other community species if they are very slow; adult males will frequently fight.

Glass Catfish *(Kryptopterus bicirrhis)*

Family: Siluridae

Distribution: Eastern India and Southeast Asia

Size: 4 inches

Food: Carnivorous

Temperature: 72 to 79 degrees Fahrenheit

Glass Catfish.

This species is one of the few aquarium catfish that does not inhabit the tank bottom. Like other midwater fish, this shoaling species should be placed with at least four of its peers. The Glass Catfish has a transparent body. Although sometimes difficult to acclimate to the aquarium, this hardy fish is a worthwhile addition to the community tank.

Bottom Fish

These fish generally belong to the catfish group, but there are other species that prefer to stay on or near the bottom. The bottom fish are usually tank cleaners, eating bottom detritus and algae. Therefore, no aquarium would be complete without a few.

Corydoras Catfish *(Corydoras species)*

Family: Callichthyidae

Distribution: South America

Size: 1.5 to 2.5 inches

Food: Omnivorous

Temperature: 72 to 79 degrees Fahrenheit

The Corydoras catfish are a genus of fish that are very similar to one another and come in many varieties. They are generally very hardy fish that feed on the substrate with their whiskerlike barbels. Popular species include the Bronze Corydoras *(Corydoras aeneus)*, the Arched Corydoras *(Corydoras arcuatus)*, Axelrod's Corydoras *(Corydoras axelrodi)*, the Leopard Corydoras *(Corydoras julii)*, and the Dusky Corydoras *(Corydoras septentrionalis)*. These fish have a flat bottom so that they can stay close to the substrate. They have an adipose fin and armored bony plates rather than scales. They tend to be nocturnal, going about their cleaning business at night. During the day, they like to find a quiet place to hide. They like to live with others of their species, so keep three to five together. Don't depend on the substrate to feed these fish; their diets should be augmented with other foods.

*Arched
Corydoras.*

Flying Fox (*Epalzeorhynchus kallopterus*)
Family: Cyprinidae
Distribution: Borneo, Indonesia, Thailand, India
Size: 6 inches
Food: Omnivorous
Temperature: 75 to 79 degrees Fahrenheit

The Flying Fox is not strictly a bottom species because it will also rest on the leaves of broad-leaved plants or graze algae on large flat stones. This species is a loner so it does not require the company of others of its kind, although several can be kept in an aquarium if ample space is provided for each to establish a territory.

Flying Fox.

Clown Loach *(Botia macracanthus)*
Family: Cobitidae
Distribution: Borneo, India
Size: 6 inches
Food: Omnivorous
Temperature: 77 to 86 degrees Fahrenheit

Clown Loach.

This uniquely colorful species of loach is an excellent addition to any community tank. It has barbels like the catfish and the same bottom cleaning propensity. It is recommended that you keep several young as a school, but only one mature adult in your aquarium.

Red-tailed Shark *(Epalzeorhynchus bicolor)*

Family: Cyprinidae
Distribution: Thailand
Size: 4.5 inches
Food: Omnivorous
Temperature: 72 to 79 degrees Fahrenheit

Red-tailed Shark.

I almost hesitate to include this species in the section on recommended species of tropical fish because of its sometimes aggressive behavior towards other tank fish. It is, however, a very popular community tank fish that is carried by many pet dealers. It is best to keep a solitary individual in your tank because these fish occupy territories which they will defend against members of their own species. Put them together only with fast small fish or with easygoing larger fish.

Clown Plecostomus *(Peckoltia arenaria)*

Family: Loricariidae
Distribution: Peru
Size: 4.5 inches
Food: Herbivorous
Temperature: 72 to 80 degrees Fahrenheit

It would difficult to cover the bottom fish without including one of the species of plecostomus. These fish are famous for their "window cleaning" abilities. This species is one of the smaller suckermouthed catfish that is ideally suited for the community tank. Others will attain lengths in excess of

10 inches and are not well suited for the beginner. This species has been known to be aggressive to its own kind, so it is best to keep only one in your aquarium. Plenty of cover and caves should be provided.

Clown Pleco.

Fish to Avoid as Beginners

There are many species of fish that are not well suited to the beginner's aquarium for a number of reasons. Some may be highly sensitive to fluctuating water quality conditions characteristic of the new aquarium. Others may require special water conditions like softer water or brackish water. The beginner should not try to provide this type of habitat without acquiring some experience. Finally, there are a number of species that are not socially compatible with the peaceful community tank. This group includes large carnivorous fish that eat smaller fish, territorial fish that do not tolerate trespassing and mature fish that display aggression and combative behavior during spawning or prespawning periods.

Many of these species are offered by the pet store and may even be promoted by the dealer because the juveniles are considered "harmless." Don't be fooled by this argument, these fish grow fast and develop aggressive attitudes early in life. The small flake-eating baby will become a neon-eating carnivore in a matter of months.

Don't be fooled into buying fish that require special water conditions. These fish may live for days or weeks in your tank, but chronic stress will set in, the fish's immune response will fail, and the fish will ultimately die from disease.

The following is a list of some species of fish that, while likely available in your aquarium store, you should avoid adding to your community aquarium.

Green Discus *(Symphysodon aequifasciatus)*

Oscar *(Astronotus ocellatus)*

Red Devil *(Amphilophus labiatus)*

Jewel Cichlid *(Hemichromis bimaculatus)*

Jack Dempsey *(Nandopsis octofasciatus)*

Runny-nose Tetra *(Hemigrammus bleheri)*

Tinfoil Barb *(Barbus schwanefeldi)*

Sucking Loach *(Gyrinocheilus aymonieri)*

Red Snakehead *(Channa micropeltes)*

Mudskipper *(Periophthalmus barbarus)*

Clown Knifefish *(Notopterus chitala)*

Arowana *(Osteoglossum bicirrhosum)*

part three
Caring for Your

Freshwater Aquarium

Feeding

Your Fish

Gold Gourami

Feeding Strategies

There are many considerations when it comes to providing food for your fish. In their natural habitat, fish have evolved various feeding strategies to optimize their ability to get nourishment. With all the different kinds of fish and habitats, you can imagine the many kinds of feeding strategies that exist, but there are some similarities. Fish can be divided into general groups based on the type of feeding strategy they use.

Carnivores

These fish are primarily predators that, in nature, feed on smaller fish or larger fish that they incapacitate. When kept in the aquarium, many of these species have been successfully fed dead food, and commercially prepared pellets and flakes. Pieces of fish, shrimp, and even bits of meat will be taken by the carnivore. Some species will simply not accept anything but live food. Guppies and goldfish are commonly offered to these predators. None of the recommended community fish outlined in chapter 5 require such measures.

Herbivores

These fish feed on vegetative matter—plants. Fish that require a diet of this nature will consume commercially prepared vegetable flakes. Their diet should be augmented with household vegetables including peas, lettuce, potatoes, beans and cauliflower. Aquarium algae will also attract the herbivore.

Insectivores

Fish with this kind of diet feed on aquatic and terrestrial invertebrates. As you would expect, these fish readily accept commercially prepared flakes and pellets, but you should also include a variety of invertebrates on top of these foods. Frozen brine shrimp and blood worms are good examples of what you can feed these fish.

It's best for the beginning aquarist to start off with omnivorous species, like the Guppies pictured here.

Omnivores

These fish will feed on a variety of foods and have no specific dietary preferences. You have probably noticed that most of the recommended species outlined in chapter 5 are omnivorous. The beginner aquarist should not have to worry about special feeding strategies when setting up a tank for the first time. These fish will accept commercially prepared flake and pellet foods, but providing a good variety of foods is necessary to meet all the dietary requirements of these fish.

Food Categories

There are basically four different categories of food: flake or dried foods; frozen or freeze-dried foods; live foods; and household foods. Of these, those that can be most harmful to your fish are the live foods. These can carry diseases or parasites that are dangerous to your fish.

Household Foods for Your Fish

Frozen (serve thawed): clams, oysters, lobster, crabmeat, shrimp, fish, mussels

Canned: the same as frozen, plus beans and peas

Raw: the same as frozen, plus ground beef, spinach, lettuce

Cooked: potato, beans, peas, egg yolk, broccoli, cauliflower, chicken

Live food and food other than flakes are highly desirable additions to your fish's diet, but remember to feed pellets or flakes as a staple. When you feed your fish table food, always serve it plain, not seasoned, salted or spiced.

Flakes or Dried Foods

Commercially prepared foods contain the three basic requirements of proteins, fats and carbohydrates. They are also supplemented with vitamins and minerals. These foods come in many varieties depending on the preferred diet, size and feeding behavior of the fish. Flakes, tablets, pellets and crumb forms are available. For example, larger predatory fish should be fed pellets as opposed to flakes because they prefer to consume a large quantity. Fish that feed on the bottom may not venture to the surface for flakes, so they must be fed pellets or tablets that will sink.

All of the community fish reviewed in this book will survive on flake foods. However, if you want active, colorful, healthy fish, you should vary their diets. Use flakes as a staple, and make every effort to substitute other foods a couple of times a week.

Live Foods

Live food is an excellent source of nutrition for your fish. Make sure you obtain live foods from your pet store, because those collected from a pond or lake may carry diseases that will affect your fish. In any event, this is a great degree easier and safer than collecting live foods yourself.

The only two live foods that generally do not run the risk of carrying a disease are earthworms and brine shrimp. These are easily obtained and will provide an excellent addition to your fish's diet. Other types of live foods that you can feed your fish include tubifex, whiteworms, *daphnia*, *drosphila* and bloodworms. Ask your pet dealer to explain the advantages and disadvantages of each, including any precautions you should take before feeding them to your fish.

Your fish need to have protein, fats, carbohydrates, vitamins, and minerals in the right amounts to be active and healthy. (Flamingo Dwarf Gourami)

Frozen or Freeze-dried Foods

This option offers the best of the live food without the risk of disease and without the hassle of preparing cultures. These include many of the live foods listed above: brine shrimp, tubifex worms, *daphnia*, and bloodworms. In addition, mosquito larvae and krill are also available to the aquarist in this form. Frozen and freeze-dried foods are a great convenience to the hobbyist who wants to provide variety without having to deal with purchasing or culturing live foods.

Table or Household Foods

Fresh, frozen or canned oysters, clams, mussels, crabmeat, lobster or bits of raw fish, are fine but do not offer canned tuna fish. Baked or boiled beans, steamed cauliflower or broccoli and boiled or baked potatoes are excellent additions to your herbivore's diet. Fresh spinach or lettuce is also good for your omnivorous and herbivorous fish. Carnivores will especially enjoy small bits of ground beef or cooked chicken.

These foods must be given in moderation. Remember, you are augmenting your fish's diet with these foods, not creating a staple. Household foods must be diced or shredded so that your fish can eat them. Don't offer your fish table scraps other than those listed above. Do not offer any bits of meat or vegetable that have been seasoned or spiced; table food needs to be plain and chopped up.

For bottom feeding fish like this Bronze Corydoras Catfish, make sure you provide pellets that sink to the bottom of the tank.

How to Feed Your Fish

The biggest problems when feeding your fish is determining how much and how often to feed them. Some fish are gluttons while others will stop when they are sated. In general, many feel that it is better to feed too little than too much to your fish. Follow the guidelines listed below when feeding your fish and you will develop a working sense of how much and how often to feed them.

1. Offer as much food as your fish will eat in five minutes. Flakes should sink no deeper than one-third the height of the tank; provide tablets or pellets for bottom fish.

2. Feed your fish in very small portions over the five-minute period.

3. If you are home during the day, feed your fish over the course of the day in small portions. If you are not home, feed you fish twice a day at the same times every day, once in the morning, once at night.

4. Always feed your fish at the same spot in the tank.

Make sure you do not overfeed your fish, no matter how much you think they need it. (Platy)

5. Don't overfeed the fish, no matter how much you think they need more food. Overeating will stress your fish and cause detritus to accumulate in the tank, degrading water quality.

Watch all your fish during feeding, making sure that each gets its share of food. Remember that fish have different mouth shapes, which allow them to feed at different levels in the tank. Some species will not go to the surface to eat and will wait for food to disperse throughout the tank. Don't rely on surface feedings and the leftovers of others to feed bottom fish. Pellets that sink to the bottom should be provided for these fish. Remember, refusal to eat is one of the first signs of illness, so keep an eye out for fish that seem to have no interest in food.

Types of Feeding Strategies

You can divide fish into three groups based on the kind of feeding strategy they use: carnivores, herbivores and omnivores. Carnivores only eat other fish and live food. Herbivores eat only vegetable matter. They will eat flake foods and other types of plant matter. Most of the fish listed in this book are omnivores. They will eat flakes, live foods and bits of table food. They are clearly the easiest group to feed and are thus most highly recommended for the beginning aquarist.

Try not to feed your fish right after turning on the light; they won't be fully alert until about thirty minutes later. In addition, don't crumble the flake food. This will add fine particles to the water that are not ingested and remain in the water degrading water quality. Your fish won't have any problems biting and grinding whole flake food.

If you are going to be away from your aquarium for up to a few days, the fish will be fine without food. For extended periods, make arrangements for someone to feed your fish or install an automatic food dispenser. If you choose the latter, be sure not to overload the dispenser, and set a long interval between feeding times so that fish will eat all that is offered.

Maintaining

Your Aquarium

You have planned your aquarium, purchased your equipment, set up your tank, established excellent water quality, carefully selected and introduced the fish, and fed them well. Now it is time to learn how to maintain the quality of their new home. Aquarium maintenance in-

volves everything from turning the light on and off everyday and feeding the fish to spending time observing the fish. This latter task is often the most enjoyable. Get to know your fish, watch how they interact and make note of any unusual behavior. Closely check the fish for any signs of disease and watch their interactions to see if any are being picked on.

The more constant you make the conditions in your aquarium, the less likely you are to cause stress to your fish. Rapid fluctuations in water temperature and water quality will cause stress and therefore compromise the health of your fish. You must monitor the water temperature, making sure that it remains constant. Examine the filter, the heater, and the airstones to make sure that they are in working order. The filter may be experiencing some blockage, especially if you are using a box filter. The thermostat light in the heater should be working properly. Make sure that the air pump and airstones are operating at maximum efficiency. These things should be checked daily and require just a few moments of your time. While you are feeding or simply enjoying your pets, you can perform a routine check of the tank components and the aquarium occupants.

Observing the fish is one of the most enjoyable tasks associated with maintaining your aquarium. (Guppies)

General Maintenance

Cleaning an aquarium involves an active, conscientious effort on your part. Maintaining a fish tank is not for the lazy at heart. Don't set up a tank if you don't intend to follow through and keep it clean and healthy. All too often, interest wanes after the first couple of months and the aquarium ultimately suffers the consequences. Realize that going into this hobby requires a real commitment. Concern must be shown at every step and on every level. Your fish's lives depend on your attention to detail.

Vacuuming

Vacuuming is one of the most important parts of maintaining your tank. You must prevent the accumulation of mulm or detritus in the gravel. Mulm is the combination of fish wastes and uneaten food that ends up on the bottom of the aquarium and decays. If not removed, this organic waste will ultimately break down into nitrites and nitrates via the nitrogen cycle. This will disturb your water chemistry, potentially harming your fish. If detritus is allowed to accumulate to excessive levels, your filter will be clogged and water quality will go downhill fast. If you have an undergravel filter, vacuuming is still very important because too much mulm will clog these filters as well, preventing water flow through the gravel.

Happy, healthy fish require tank maintenance and attention from you, the fishkeeper (Gold Angelfish)

Aquarium vacuums are available from your pet dealer. I recommend using a wide hose to siphon wastes while you are doing a water change. This in effect accomplishes two goals at once: vacuuming mulm and removing water from the tank.

Check the Filter

Assuming you have an external filter or a box filter, it is very important to check the filter media. The top level mat gets dirty quickly and easily, as this is the level that collects the largest pieces of debris. An excessive buildup of detritus in your filter will inhibit flow and ultimately reduce the filter's effectiveness.

Rinse the filter mat under lukewarm water every three or four months until the water is clear. You should probably replace about 50 percent of the media every six months, making sure to reuse about half of the old filter material. You have established a viable working bacterial colony in your filter medium and you don't want to throw it out and start from square one. That's why some of the old media must be retained. One of the most common mistakes is the replacement of the entire filter contents every couple of months because it looks dirty. Some of that "dirt" is bacteria that's beneficial to the filtering process. For filters that utilize cartridges as media, check with the manufacturer for optimum maintenance and replacement rate.

Algae

What exactly is algae and do all algae cause problems for your tank? Algae are actually plants that belong to the class known as Thallophyta, the same class as fungi. They are relatively simple plants that range in size from the one-celled microscopic types to large seaweeds that grow to over 230 feet. Algae are also very hardy plants that have a tremendous reproductive capacity. They can enter your aquarium as airborne algal spores or can be carried by snails and tank furnishings from another aquarium.

Most species of algae occur in the waters and, like fish, have adapted to all kinds of water conditions. In your aquarium, they can be found on the surface, suspended in the water or on the surfaces of rocks, gravel and tank decorations.

In low levels, algae can be somewhat beneficial to the aquarium, providing the same benefits as plants. But if algae is present, it will generally grow in excess if the right conditions exist. Excessive algal growth will overrun a tank unless water quality is properly maintained. High nitrate levels and sunlight will promote algal growth. Avoiding these conditions will minimize algae as a tank nuisance.

If you seem to have excessive algal growth, there are several measures you can employ to reduce the presence of algae in the aquarium.

- The introduction of algae eaters like Flying Foxes, Black Mollies, and Corydoras Catfish will serve to keep algae in check on gravel, rocks and plants.

- Reduce the duration of light to ten hours per day instead of twelve hours.

- Make sure that all rocks, decorations and gravel going into the tank are free of algae.

- Scrape algae from the aquarium walls with an algae scraper. These are usually either sponges attached to a long stick, a razor blade attached to a stick or magnetic scrapers.

- Remove excess nitrates, which will fuel algal growth by carrying out partial water changes in a timely fashion.

Don't become obsessed with algae to the point where you feel that all algae must be removed from the aquarium. I guarantee you that this is simply something that can't be effectively done. Expect to live with a little algae in your tank.

Test the Water

When you first set up the aquarium, testing the water every couple of days is critical to the water maturation process. When you begin to add fish, water chemistry changes radically, and water quality monitoring is critical to the survival of your fish. After this sensitive period of two to four weeks, it is still very important to test your water, and I recommend that you do so every week for the first two months. This will give you a good understanding of the mechanics of the nitrogen cycle and will indicate to you when the nitrates are to the point where a water change is needed.

After two months, your tank will certainly be well established and the need to test the water every week will diminish. At this point, a monthly water test will suffice unless you suspect that you might have tank problems. Sudden behavioral changes in your fish, fish disease, fish mortality, excessive algal growth, "smelly" water and cloudy water all warrant an immediate water quality test and possible water change.

Water Changes

Water changes are one of the most important aspects of cleaning and maintaining your tank. A water change is when you literally take out a percentage of the aquarium water and replace it with fresh or distilled water. The amount you change varies with the quality of your tank and with the frequency of water changes. Some experts feel that 10 percent water change is sufficient every week, while others feel that this volume should be closer to 30 percent. I recommend that you start with a water change of 10 to 20 percent every week and raise or lower this amount depending on water quality.

Water changes help to maintain good water quality because you are diluting the amount of nitrogenous compounds like nitrites and nitrates, harmful gases, and other toxic substances each time you do one. The water you add, which should be pure distilled water if possible, will be more oxygen rich than the water in your tank.

The best way to do a water change is to use a siphon and a large bucket. The siphon is basically just a 3- or 4-foot hose or tube that will transfer water from the tank to the bucket.

How to Siphon

1. Fill the tube completely with water making sure there is no trapped air anywhere in the tube. Make sure that the siphon is clean and that your hands are clean as well. You can fill the hose at the sink or by submerging it in the aquarium. Only do the latter if your aquarium is large enough to accommodate the hose without spooking the fish. Use your thumbs to block both ends of the siphon to keep the water in and air out.

2. Keeping your thumbs in place, place one end of the hose in the aquarium and aim the other at the bucket. Make sure that the bucket end is lower than the aquarium or siphoning will not work. If you filled your siphon in the aquarium, plug one end of the hose tightly, lift it from the aquarium, and lower it to the bucket.

3. Release your thumbs and the water will begin to flow rapidly from the aquarium into the bucket.

As I mentioned earlier, use the siphon to remove debris from the tank while you are making a water change. When it is time to add water and if distilled water is not available, use tap water that you have allowed to age for one or two days. Either keep a few 1-gallon jugs stored in the house or keep a 5-gallon bucket filled with water for a couple of days. Make sure that the water you add is close in temperature to that of your aquarium.

There are now devices that can be attached to your tank that will change the water for you on a constant basis. Whether you have chlorinated water or not, your pet store will be able to equip you with one of these water changers. It makes life much easier but requires that you have a faucet constantly available somewhere near the aquarium. Water changers are labor-saving devices that make maintenance much easier and life better for your fish.

Maintenance Checklist

Daily

- Feed the fish twice a day.

- Turn the tank lights on and off.

- Check the water temperature.

- Check the heater and make sure the thermostat light is working.

- Make sure the filter(s) are working properly.

- Make sure the aerator is working properly.

Weekly

- Study the fish closely, watching for behavioral changes and signs of disease.

- Change approximately 10 to 20 percent of the aquarium water.

- Add distilled or aged water to compensate for water evaporation.

- Check the filter to see if the top mat needs to be replaced.

- Vacuum the tank thoroughly and attempt to clean up mulm and detritus.

- Test the water for pH, nitrates, softness (first two months).

- Trim and fertilize aquarium plants as needed.

Monthly

- Change 25 percent of the aquarium water.

- Clean the tank's inside glass with an algae scraper.

- Vacuum the tank thoroughly, stirring up the gravel and eliminating mulm.

- Test the water for pH, nitrates and softness.

- Rinse any tank decorations that suffer from dirt buildup.

- Trim and fertilize plants; replace plants if necessary.

Quarterly

- Change 50 percent of the water; replace with distilled or aged water.

- Replace airstones.

- Rinse the filter materials completely and replace some of them if necessary.

- Clean the inside aquarium glass with an algae scraper.

- Vacuum the tank thoroughly, stirring up the gravel and eliminating mulm.

- Trim and fertilize plants as needed; replace if necessary.

- Test the water for pH, nitrates and softness.

- Rinse any tank decorations that suffer from dirt buildup.

Yearly

- Strip down the filter; replace at least 50 percent of the media with new mat and charcoal.

- Replace the airstones.

- Wash the gravel entirely.

- Clean the inside of the tank thoroughly.

- Restart the aquarium all over again, but save some of the original aquarium water to help condition the tank.

Keeping Your Fish
Healthy

Freshwater tropical fish are subject to all kinds of maladies. Pathogenic organisms including parasites, bacteria and viruses are present in all aquariums. Many are introduced with new fish and many are highly contagious. However, whether or not diseases actually break out depends on the resistance of your fish. Poor living conditions will weaken your fish, cause chronic stress, and ultimately lower the fish's resistance. This is why I have repeatedly stressed the importance of maintaining a healthy aquarium for you pets. Even if you do everything in your power to maintain a disease-free aquarium, you may find yourself confronting health conditions in your fish; even experts fall victim to these problems.

Signs of Illness

The first step to treating any kind of ailment in your aquarium is to recognize and identify the problem. You will be able to determine that a fish is not healthy by its appearance and its behavior. Since you have been spending time examining your fish while you feed them, you will be able to identify problems as soon as they manifest themselves. Telltale behavioral symptoms include: no desire to eat; hyperventilation of the gills; gasping for air near the surface; erratic swimming behavior; lack of movement; rubbing of body or fins; and twitching of fins.

External symptoms include a variety of physical abnormalities of the head, body, fins, gills, scales and anus. As I review the various diseases associated with aquarium fish, you will learn what the symptoms of each are.

The Hospital Tank

In an earlier chapter, I mentioned that some aquarists isolate new fish in a quarantine tank. This way, the fish can be evaluated for signs of disease before introduction into the main aquarium. For your community tank, I didn't recommend a quarantine tank because of the complexities associated with having to maintain two aquariums.

The aquarist should do everything possible to maintain a clean, disease-free aquarium.

Many experts recommend that you set up a hospital tank to isolate individuals that are suffering from disease. This tank will reduce the likelihood of the disease spreading to others in the aquarium. It will provide refuge to a fish that may ordinarily be harassed by healthier fish. The hospital tank will make it easier to treat the fish without subjecting other fish to the treatment. And it will make it easier to observe and diagnose the ailing fish.

As your expertise in this hobby increases, you will start to accumulate more expensive fish that you simply do not want to risk with disease. At this point, a hospital tank will be mandatory. It will also act as a quarantine tank, provided that it has not recently housed a diseased fish.

The hospital tank need not be large; a 10-gallon tank will do. It does need adequate filtration and aeration, but plants and gravel should be left out. Try to provide some kind of cover for the fish in the form of rocks or flower pots as a source of security.

Spend time observing your fish so you'll be alerted to possible diseases and conditions as soon as possible.

Treatments

It is very important that beginners use commercially available treatments instead of homemade remedies. Some experts recommend chemicals like malachite green or potassium permanganate. These chemicals must be handled in very exact dosages. If a fish is overdosed with one of them, it will kill the fish faster than the disease would have. Discuss all the possible remedies to a disease with your local pet dealer and let that person advise you on the best commercial remedies the store carries. If you are still not satisfied, don't be afraid to call your veterinarian and ask a few questions. If your veterinarian does not handle fish, he or she can usually recommend somebody who does. Finally, when you apply the remedy, make sure that you follow the directions exactly.

The Old-fashioned Salt Bath

This is the most time-tested cure-all of the fish world. Sometimes called the progressive saltwater treatment, it is what the hospital tank most often stands for. This very simple treatment has been known to cure a number of fish diseases including ich, fungus, velvet and tail rot.

You simply add 1 teaspoon of table salt (not iodized) for each gallon of water to the hospital tank which houses your fish. Add the same amount of salt that night and twice the next day, again in the morning and at night. If there are not improvements by the third or fourth day, add one more teaspoon of salt each day. On the ninth and tenth days, make progressive water changes and check for results.

Emergency Cleaning

This is the most severe treatment any tank can get. If any of the infestations mentioned in the following pages strike more than three or four fish, you need to take drastic measures and perform an emergency cleaning. Place all the fish in the hospital tank and begin treatment. Then, turn your attention to the aquarium.

This very simply involves starting your aquarium from scratch. It must be thoroughly cleaned and totally restarted. Throw out filter media and save as little as possible. Empty out the contents of the tank. Rinse the walls, the gravel and the filter with bleach. Of course, make sure that you rinse everything thoroughly. Do the same to the plastic plants. Throw out the rocks and buy new ones. If you have any live plants, dispose of them too, and don't use them for any other purpose. Replace the filter media and airstones, etc. Take the heater and wash it with bleach as well, making sure to rinse it thoroughly. In essence, you are starting over again because your tank was overrun by disease.

Common Conditions

There are literally hundreds of possible maladies that can afflict fish. Some are specific to certain species and some can easily be transferred between species. Not all are common in the average home aquarium. The causes of common aquarium ailments may be bacteria, viruses, fungi or parasites. The following provides a general overview of those diseases you are most likely to encounter in your aquarium. For a more complete listing of tropical fish diseases and their treatments, consult the references in chapter 10.

CONSTIPATION OR INDIGESTION (NOT CONTAGIOUS)

A fish that is constipated or suffering from indigestion is often inactive and usually rests on the bottom of the tank. In addition, its abdomen generally swells or bulges. This can be caused by an incorrect diet, food that doesn't agree with the fish, or overfeeding. You will need to change the food you are feeding the fish. Some experts add 1 teaspoon of Epsom salts for each 5 gallons of water in the hospital tank. Starve the fish for three to five days until it returns to being active. When it resumes normal behavior, feed it live or freeze-dried food for one whole week. After one week, return the fish to its normal tank. This is a problem that tends to recur, so make it a point to watch this fish.

Swim bladder disease can result from bruising during fighting or breeding. These two Kissing Gourami could be at risk, as they are actually having a heated dispute.

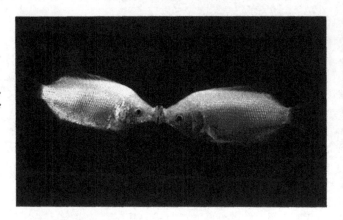

SWIM BLADDER PROBLEMS (NOT CONTAGIOUS)

This is fairly easy to diagnose because the fish can't swim properly. It suffers from a loss of balance, swimming on its sides or upside down, or sometimes somersaulting through the water. Swim bladder disease can result from constipation, from bruising of the swim bladder during handling, fighting, breeding or from bacterial infection associated with poor water quality. These problems have been known to correct themselves as the bruised area heals, but you can't always count on this. If you suspect a bacterial infection, improve water quality and treat the fish with a broad-spectrum antibiotic. If this problem is associated with constipation, your fish is more likely to experience a recurrence. Feed your fish something else, as diet can be one of the biggest reasons this disease develops.

DROPSY OR KIDNEY BLOAT (MAY BE CONTAGIOUS)

This is also known as "pinecone" disease because the belly bloats noticeably and the scales stick out like a pinecone. In general, this disease causes the body to swell due to a buildup of fluid in the tissues. This disease is thought to be caused by water quality problems or some kind of organ failure. Fish generally don't live more than a week after full-blown dropsy makes itself known. Like constipation and swim bladder disease, fish that survive dropsy tend to have recurring attacks. While dropsy is not thought to be contagious, it is best to remove the fish at once. The tank should receive an emergency cleaning.

Many experts still feel that dropsy is not treatable and that the fish should be immediately removed and painlessly destroyed. Others feel that medicated food is one way to treat dropsy. Still others suggest mixing Furanace with water, 250 milligrams to the gallon. This bath should last only one hour and should not be repeated more than three times in three days. It is thought that Furanace can be absorbed by the fish through the skin. If you choose not to use this remedy, you can always try the old-fashioned salt bath (see above). If your fish does not respond to treatment in two or three days, it should probably be humanely destroyed.

TUMORS (USUALLY NOT CONTAGIOUS)

Obvious lumps, bumps or protrusions, tumors sometimes look like a large blister or wart. They have been known to grow to the size of a large screw head. They can be surgically removed, but only by a veterinarian.

POP-EYE (EXOPHTHALMUS; NOT CONTAGIOUS)

This disease causes the eyes to bulge from their sockets and is, therefore, easy to recognize in most tropical fish. The condition is generally caused by poor water quality and the subsequent chronic stress. Recovery may take several days if efforts are made to improve the water quality. Some feel that food should be withheld for two or three days until tank conditions are corrected.

Bacterial, Viral and Fungal Infections

FURUNCULOSIS (ULCER DISEASE)

This bacterial infection will go unnoticed for some time, but then it will spread rapidly. These bacteria infect the flesh under the scales somewhat like skin flukes (see below). However, this infection is first manifested by the appearance of bumps underneath the scales. A short time later, the bumps rupture and create large bleeding ulcers. That is why this ailment is sometimes referred to as "ulcer disease." There is no certain cure for this.

While some fish have actually survived, large scars resulting from the infection often prove a problem for them. Fish with these kinds of ulcers should probably be destroyed. The remaining fish should be treated with tetracycline immediately. Some experts argue that all foods should be immediately changed and that any remaining existing foods be disposed of. Tetracycline treatment can last up to ten days. You may want to elevate your aquarium temperature to 80 degrees Fahrenheit for that time if you do not have any fish that are intolerant of high temperatures. Furunculosis is a cold-water disease and the high temperature is thought to kill it.

ULCERS (HOLE-IN-THE-BODY DISEASE; HIGHLY CONTAGIOUS)

This is an infection that tends to be internal and that manifests itself in large red ulcers, boils and dark reddening at the bases of the fins. It cannot be mistaken for anchor worm because anchor-worm ulcers swell up, whereas these tend to eat away into the body.

A salt bath may be too harsh, but the infected fish should be isolated immediately and fed medicated food. At times, antibiotics are required and you will need a veterinarian for this. Consult your local pet store before proceeding.

FUNGUS (HIGHLY CONTAGIOUS)

The most common species of fungus infecting tropical fish is *Saprolegnia*. It is a fuzzy growth that is different from velvet because it is whiter and easier to notice. The primary cause of this infection is damage to the mucous layer on the skin. This allows fungal spores to germinate and grow into the skin. Injury, environmental conditions, and parasites can damage the protective mucous layer.

Some experts treat this fungus with methylene blue which they paint on the infected areas. This fish is then placed in a ten-day salt water treatment. Again, commercial remedies are also available and the entire aquarium should be treated with a fungicide.

Many tropical fish diseases are highly contagious, so it is necessary for the infected fish to be isolated in a hospital tank as soon as possible.

BODY SLIME FUNGUS (HIGHLY CONTAGIOUS)

This deadly affliction can kill your fish in two days if not caught in time. The protective mucous coating grows white and starts peeling off as if the fish were shedding its skin. The fins are gradually covered as well. Eventually, the body becomes red with irritation.

Do not hesitate to call your pet store immediately. Commercial remedies are available, but must be administered quickly. A salt bath with warm temperatures may be a temporary solution, as it should retard growth of the fungus. However, a cure must be found and a salt bath won't do it; though some have found that severe salt treatments with ich cures are effective.

MOUTH FUNGUS (COLUMNARIS DISEASE; CONTAGIOUS)

This disease is caused by the bacteria *Flexibacter* and manifests itself as a white cottony growth on the mouth. It can happen on the gills, back and fins. If left untreated for any length of time, this infection will destroy the entire infected region and lead to eventual death.

Commercial cures are available, but you can begin by isolating the fish and administering the salt water treatment. Some aquarists will start with a salt bath and then use a general fungal or bacterial control. Consult with your pet store once you have diagnosed the problem.

FISH POX (PROBABLY NOT CONTAGIOUS)

This disease affects goldfish, koi, and carp more than it does other aquarium fish, but it should be covered in this chapter. This is a viral infection that causes milky white or pinkish gray waxy film to develop over the fish's skin and fins. The usual pattern is that it appears, gets worse, and then disappears.

It is not definitively known what triggers fish pox and what eventually happens. However, it does not appear to be contagious. Nonetheless, take the necessary precautions and isolate the infected fish until the film goes away. This will generally take seven to ten days. This ailment is more annoying then anything else since it does not kill the fish. However, there is no known cure.

FIN OR TAIL ROT (CONTAGIOUS)

This is sometimes caused by fighting among your fish—the fins get damaged and then bacteria infect the injured area. It can also be triggered by poor water quality. It is easily detectable as the fins have missing parts and eventually become shredded. As the disease worsens, the entire fin will be eaten away. There are many broad-spectrum medications that will help you deal with this situation. Consult your local pet store dealer.

Some experts argue that the best way to treat the infection is by dipping your fish for five minutes in a bath made up of eight crystals of potassium permanganate to three quarts of water. Then you cut off the infected areas of the tail or fin and paint them with methylene blue or Mercurochrome. Steps like this may be for experts only.

Be sure to treat the aquarium water as well because fin rot is usually contagious. Also, take the steps necessary to remedy the cause of the infection. Separate fish that cause injury to the fins and make sure water quality is at its best.

CHINA DISEASE (HIGHLY CONTAGIOUS)

This is not a very common disease, and you must be absolutely certain of your diagnosis. This is the most contagious disease listed here, and it is the most deadly. There is no known cure for China disease.

The symptoms are very easy to diagnose. The tail fin and other fins begin to fray, very much as in fin rot. However, with China disease it begins at the base of the fin and works its way outward. Also, the infected areas begin to blacken. Even the ventral region begins to turn black.

Unfortunately, the infected fish must be painlessly destroyed and the other fish put in the hospital tank. A ten-day progressive salt treatment is a good idea.

In the meantime, you need to perform an emergency cleaning in the tank. This must be done immediately to prevent further damage by this disease.

Parasite Infestations

FISH LICE (HIGHLY CONTAGIOUS)

Fish lice are parasitic crustaceans of the species *Argulus* that are very easy to recognize on the surface of your fish. They are round, disk-shaped crustaceans with prominent eyes, sucking disks and a stiletto mouthpart that clamps firmly onto its host. They can move about the host with ease and tend to take on the color of the fish that they parasitize. Often the infected fish will rub up against objects in the tank in an effort to scrape these pests off. Some fish have been known to jump out of the water in an attempt to cleanse themselves of these parasites. These creatures feed by sucking the blood and tissue fluids out of the fish through the skin and scales. Sometimes they occur on the fins, but this is not as satisfying for them. Fish lice can also transmit other microscopic diseases and wounds may develop secondary bacterial infections.

Fortunately, there are a number of high quality commercially produced products out on the market to control parasites. Your local pet dealer can help you select one. The fish should be quarantined and the tank disinfected with the same parasite control.

ANCHOR WORM (HIGHLY CONTAGIOUS)

These elongated crustaceans of the genus *Lernaea* also attach to the skin of the fish. Several species of this parasite have been described, but all females have a head with an anchor shape that embeds in the flesh of the host. The fish will rub against anything it can in an attempt to scrape off the parasite. Like fish lice, these creatures cause irritation and localized bleeding at the point of attachment; from this protrudes a white worm that can sometimes grow quite long. Secondary bacterial infection can occur at these points.

Treatment of the anchor worm will include taking the fish out of the water and removing the worm with forceps or tweezers.

To remove the worm: Place a wet cloth in your hand. Take hold of the fish in the hand holding the cloth. Make sure to position the fish so that the worm is facing you. With a pair of household tweezers, press as close to the ulcer as possible, but only extract the worm. Make sure not to rip any flesh off the fish and be careful not to break the parasite. This is very dangerous to the fish and you must be extremely cautious when approaching this. It may be best to get someone experienced to do it for you.

As in the case with fish lice, be sure to treat the infected area with an antiseptic after removing the parasite. In addition, antibiotic treatment may accelerate the healing of lesions; consult your dealer for a general full-spectrum antibiotic.

LEECHES (HIGHLY CONTAGIOUS)

Leeches are another group of parasites that may be found on the skin and scales of your fish. These are not the leeches we see as freeliving creatures in lakes and ponds. These are parasitic, wormlike creatures that attach at both ends to your fish, feeding on flesh and blood. They need to be removed as quickly as possible, but not with forceps or tweezers. These parasites are very strong and you are likely to do more damage to your fish than to the leeches by trying to pull them off. Call your pet store for advice for commercially produced cures.

Another solution involves preparing a salt bath with 8 level teaspoons of salt for each gallon of water. Once the salt is sufficiently dissolved, add the fish for no more than ten minutes. The leeches that do not fall off should be able to be removed with tweezers very easily.

Again, the aquarium needs to be treated immediately with commercially produced chemicals for parasite control. Check all your fish for parasites when one is discovered, and always isolate the infected fish.

FLUKES—SKIN AND GILL (HIGHLY CONTAGIOUS)

Like all infestations, weakened fish fall victim first. The gill fluke *(Dactylogyrus)* is very easily detectable. It causes the gills to swell up pink and red, and the fish spends a lot of time near the surface trying to suck in air. Sometimes, a pus-like fluid will be exuded from the gills at this time. These flukes are microscopic parasites that lodge themselves in the gills. Other symptoms include severe color loss, scratching and labored respiration. The skin fluke *(Gyrodactylus)* causes localized swelling, excessive mucus and ulcerations.

As with all other parasitic manifestations, the host fish is constantly trying to rub itself against objects to scrape off the infestation. Again, pet stores have pest-control remedies for this problem, which is more easily treatable than the ones I have already listed. Be sure to treat the tank as well to make sure that this parasite does not spread.

Some experts recommend a formaldehyde bath. Do this only if commercial solutions are unavailable or are not effective. Place the fish in a gallon of water. Add 15 drops of formaldehyde every minute for ten minutes. Then remove the fish and place it in a hospital tank. Repeat this process daily for three days. Formaldehyde will kill your fish, so do not haphazardly administer this chemical. Follow the instructions and time it precisely.

ICH (WHITE SPOT; HIGHLY CONTAGIOUS)

Raised white spots about the size of salt granules that appear on the body are the parasite *Ichthyophthirius*. This is one of the most common parasites among aquarium fish. It should not be taken lightly, as it will kill your fish if left untreated for too long.

This ailment is so common that there are many commercial ich remedies on the market, so don't buy the cheapest one, buy the best. Follow standard procedures and remove the fish with symptoms and treat it in a hospital tank. However, the entire aquarium must be treated as well. Follow the directions carefully.

If an ich treatment is not available to you, raise the aquarium temperature to 85 degrees Fahrenheit and add 1 teaspoon of salt for every gallon of water in the tank. Give the infected fish in the hospital tank the ten-day salt water treatment. It is important to kill this organism before it has an opportunity to infest the entire population.

VELVET (HIGHLY CONTAGIOUS)

The parasite *Oodinium* causes a golden velvety coat on the body and fins which is referred to as velvet. In orange fish, like goldfish, velvet can be difficult to detect at first. Commercially produced remedies are best for this parasitic affliction. Some experts use malachite green or the old-fashioned ten-day salt bath. Use the commercial product, but if one is not available, try the salt bath. You should administer some kind of antifungal chemical in the water of the aquarium to disinfect the tank as well.

HOLE-IN-THE-HEAD DISEASE (CONTAGIOUS)

This disease is caused by the parasite *Hexamita*, which is an internal parasite that is harmful when the fish is weakened by stress, age or poor water quality. It is generally characterized by white stringy feces and enlarged pus-filled sensory pores in the head. Other symptoms include erosion of the skin and muscles that eventually extends to the bones and skull. The lateral line is also a common site for these lesions.

Sometimes transferring the fish to larger tanks and implementing frequent water changes is enough to cure the fish. Improved nutrition supplemented with vitamin C has been known to improve the condition as well. The prescription drug metronidazole prepared in a bath of 50 milligrams for every gallon of water is effective at treating this disease. It is recommended that you repeat this treatment after three days.

part four

Beyond
the Basics

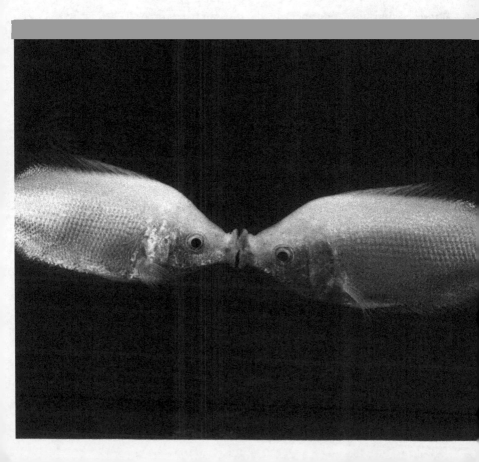

chapter

9

Resources

Home aquarists throughout the world number in the millions. As long as you have an aquarium, you will never be alone in this hobby. As you become more involved in aquarium keeping, you will be surprised at how many people share this avocation. I found myself going to my local pet dealer just to see new fish arrivals, to talk about aquarium problems and to exchange ideas with fellow aquarists. I picked up some of the most valuable information on fishkeeping from amateurs who enjoy the thrills of this hobby.

Clubs

In many areas, aquarium enthusiasts have formed clubs and associations where ideas and techniques are endlessly bantered about. Find these organizations by asking your local pet dealer if one exists in your area. Not only are these kinds of organizations great for gathering information, but they may also help you find and buy used equipment as well as healthy homebred fish.

Books

Literally thousands of books have been published on every facet of aquarium keeping. The bibliography in chapter 10 is a mere smattering of what is available for the new and experienced aquarist. Each one of the books listed has its own bibliography, which will help you to delve further into the field. Books have been written to address virtually every aspect of the hobby. They cover broad topics like basic aquarium setup to very specialized topics like the proper husbandry of a certain species. If you have any questions about aquarium keeping, they are covered in a book.

Magazines

Monthly aquarium magazines provide you with some of the most up-to-date information on aquarium keeping. Timely articles on breeding, feeding, disease and species specific husbandry will both entertain and inform the new aquarist. Product information and classified advertising are excellent features of the aquarium magazine. Two such magazines that have proven to be very good conduits of information are *Aquarium Fish Magazine* (P.O. Box 53351, Boulder, CO 80322, 303-666-8504) and *Tropical Fish Hobbyist* (One TFH Plaza, Neptune City, NJ 07753, 908-988-8400).

Fish on the Internet

Yes, even fishkeeping has entered the computer age. This is probably the fastest way to obtain and exchange information on aquarium keeping. If you have access to the Internet, then you have unlimited access to a vast amount of information on this hobby. Some Internet access companies have even established networks for fish enthusiasts. One such network is Fishnet by CompuServe (800-524-3388). Membership in this network gives you access to hobbyists, professional aquarists, researchers, breeders and vendors of aquarium products. You can even get immediate advice from staff about sick fish.

This is just one example of what is available to the aquarist on the Internet. There are also bulletin board systems for aquarists, and some experts and vendors have home pages on the Internet. Any good search machine will help you access these resources.

Bibliography

Axelrod, H. R. *Tropical Fish as a New Pet.* Neptune City, N.J.: TFH Publications Inc., 1991.

———. *Encyclopedia of Tropical Fishes: With Special Emphasis on Techniques of Breeding.* Neptune City, N.J.: TFH Publications Inc., 1986.

Axelrod, H. R. and L. P. Schultz. *Handbook of Tropical Aquarium Fishes.* Neptune City, N.J.: TFH Publications Inc., 1990.

Bailey, M. and G. Sandford. *The Ultimate Aquarium.* New York: Smithmark Publishers, 1995.

DeVito, C. and G. Skomal. *The Goldfish: An Owner's Guide to a Happy Healthy Pet.* New York: Howell Book House, 1996.

Eschmeyer, W. M. *Catalogue of the Genera of Recent Fishes.* San Francisco: California Academy of Sciences, 1990.

Emmens, C. W. *Tropical Fish: A Complete Introduction.* Neptune City, N.J.: TFH Publications Inc., 1987.

Freise, U. E. *Aquarium Fish.* Neptune City, N.J.: TFH Publications Inc., 1989.

Halstead, B. W. and B. L. Landa. *Tropical Fish.* New York: Golden Press, 1985.

James, B. *A Fishkeeper's Guide to Aquarium Plants.* London: Salamander Books, 1986.

Mills, D. *Aquarium Fish.* New York: Dorling Kindersley Publishing, 1993.

Moyle, P. B. and J. J. Cech, Jr. *Fishes: An Introduction to Ichthyology.* Englewood Cliffs, N.J.: Prentice-Hall Inc., 1982.

Sandford, G. *An Illustrated Encyclopedia of Aquarium Fish.* New York: Howell Book House, 1995.

Scheurmann, I. *The New Aquarium Handbook.* Hauppauge, N.Y.: Barron's, 1986.

————. *Water Plants in the Aquarium.* Hauppauge, N.Y.: Barron's, 1987.

Scott, P. W. *The Complete Aquarium.* New York: Dorling Kindersley Publishing, 1995.

Stadelmann, P. *Tropical Fish: A Complete Pet Owner's Manual.* Hauppauge, N.Y.: Barron's, 1991.

Stoskopf, M. K. *Fish Medicine.* Philadelphia: W.B. Saunders Co., 1993.

Printed in the USA
CPSIA information can be obtained
at www.ICGtesting.com
JSHW012012140824
68134JS00023B/2374